Toby and Sox

Toby and Sox

The heartwarming tale of a little boy with autism and a dog in a million

VIKKY TURNER
with Kate Moore

EBURY
PRESS

3 5 7 9 10 8 6 4

Ebury Press, an imprint of Ebury Publishing
20 Vauxhall Bridge Road
London SW1V 2SA

Ebury Press is part of the Penguin Random House group of companies
whose addresses can be found at global.penguinrandomhouse.com

Penguin
Random House
UK

First published by Ebury Press in 2016

www.eburypublishing.co.uk

A CIP catalogue record for this book is available from the British Library

ISBN 9781785032004

Typeset in India by Thomson Digital Pvt Ltd, Noida, Delhi
Printed and bound in Great Britain by Clays Ltd, St Ives PLC

Penguin Random House is committed to a
sustainable future for our business, our readers
and our planet. This book is made from Forest
Stewardship Council® certified paper.

For Sox, for changing our lives

'*Every once in a while a dog enters your life
and changes everything …*'

Anon

Contents

Prologue

The summer I was sixteen, I fell head over heels in love. The object of my affection had a fine set of white teeth and an affinity for ball games, and there was something in the way he stared at me with his deep-brown eyes that told me he would never let me down and would always be there for me. He was gorgeous, athletic and fun-loving, with glossy blond hair I could have stroked for hours.

His name was Dusty, and he was a Golden Retriever.

He belonged to a young man named Neil Turner and – in the beginning, at least – it was probably fair to say I was more interested in the dog than the man. But without that loyal and faithful hound, Neil and I might never have got together.

That was the first time a dog changed my life – *saved* my life, in a way.

It wouldn't be the last.

I

Family Affair

'You remember Neil, don't you, Vikky?'

I looked up from where I was sat on the sofa in Mrs Turner's living room. I had the Turners' cat, Sophie, nestled on my lap, and was fondling Dusty's golden ears with my fingers as he sat faithfully by my side. The Turners were old family friends – a friendship forged when Mrs Turner, who had been my primary school teacher when I was eight, once put me on detention for talking too much, and she and my mum had met after school to discuss my chatterbox tendencies. From this unlikeliest of scenarios a friendship blossomed, and as a child I'd sometimes played football with the Turners' son, Neil, in their back garden, as our mothers talked. But Neil was a few years older than me, and it had been several years now since I'd seen him properly. I remembered him as the bus monitor from my lower school – a kind, gentle boy, who, when a girl was once injured, had stepped up and immediately said, 'I'll carry her home,' and he did. He had a heart of gold, but since he'd moved on to the upper school and his A levels, I'd hardly seen him.

I barely recognised him now. At eighteen, Neil Turner was a man. That summer of 1988 he walked into his parents' lounge dressed in his tennis kit, all long-limbed and athletic, and somehow seemed to bring the glorious sunshine glowing outside in with him. He had brown tousled hair and a boyish grin that reached his green eyes. He grinned at me as I sat on the sofa, and seemed to be as taken aback as I was at the transformation before him. I was sixteen then, and looked rather different from the gawky schoolgirl he used to monitor on the bus. These days I had bobbed brown hair and teenage curves, and for a beat or two we just smiled at each other, before I ducked my head and turned my attention back to Dusty's floppy ears. I could feel my heart hammering suddenly in my chest. I'd felt a connection, immediate, like love at first sight, and its power was somewhat disconcerting.

Dusty, meanwhile, panted by my side, beaming at me with his doggy teeth and lolling pink tongue, and seeming to encourage me with every breath he took.

Nonetheless, if it wasn't for my little brother, Nicholas, that fleeting glimpse of Neil in his tennis kit might have been it. It was the summer I'd completed my GCSEs, and the empty, long hot months stretched before me, with all their potential for lazy days and lie-ins. But I was an attentive sister, and I got up early every day to walk Nicholas to his school bus stop. My brother was four years younger than me, and his learning difficulties meant he attended a special school. He didn't have a 'label' as such – there weren't really labels back then, the way there are today – but he'd always struggled to succeed in a mainstream school and so from a very early age he'd received special educational help. And help from me, too; I was often the only one who could get him to do some schoolwork as we sat together at the kitchen table, him battling to form his letters and do his sums. Walking him to the bus stop was just another way I could help.

As it turned out, Neil had noticed my daily sortie to the bus stop. And so, that summer, after our acquaintance had been renewed in his parents' lounge, I suddenly found that he and his dog happened to be out for their daily stroll whenever Nicholas and I were walking to the bus stop. We would 'just happen' to meet. (Neil later confessed to me that he and Dusty walked in circles – *lots* of circles – that summer in his effort to cross our path.)

It would always go the same way. Dusty would bound up to me, with his tail wagging and his doggy mouth grinning, like Cilla Black in a blonde fur coat. He was a truly lovely dog, just adorable. In his mind, the world was full of 53 million friends he hadn't met yet, but every walk gave him an opportunity to try. After I gave him lots of fuss, my eyes would travel along the lead attached to his collar, to where Neil stood behind him, patiently waiting for me to finish greeting his dog, a shy smile playing over his lips. And then he'd ask if I wanted to come with him to walk the dog, and the two of us would fall into step, with Dusty leading the way. We'd walk round and round the small village we lived in, Scraptoft in Leicestershire, until we knew every path like the back of our hands, talking nineteen to the dozen as the summer sun warmed our skin.

That connection I'd felt in the living room was still there. It really was love at first sight; there is no other way to explain it – that's just how it was. As we talked, we discovered we had the same aims and values in life. And we got on really well; we never argued. When we were apart, we missed each other like crazy – and when you miss being with someone, a *lot*, then you know you're meant to be with them. For me, from the moment we started walking that wonderful dog together, I didn't think there was any question that we were going to be anything else but together. Forever. It was a done deal, just like that.

And so, that summer, for all those glorious weeks, Neil asked me out on dates and we courted, in an old-fashioned way, and I watched him play tennis and cricket and all kinds of other sports too. I told him about the Youth Training Scheme I was going to do, come September; I had a placement at an all-girls' school as a teaching assistant, the first step in a career I was hoping to forge in child development. The thing I knew above all else was that I wanted to work with children – I loved everything about them, and I think helping my younger brother had probably inspired me too.

In turn, Neil told me all about his plans: he would be off to Leeds University at the start of the academic year to study electrical engineering as part of a three-year degree. Three years seemed an awfully long time, and Leeds an awfully long way from Scraptoft. But we made it work. Every other weekend I travelled up to Leeds to see him, and we kept the flame of our budding relationship burning bright. Nevertheless, it was hard, and I missed him desperately.

One wintry weekend in the early months of 1989, during the second term of Neil's first year, my latest visit to Leeds drew to a close. As all Sundays were back then, it was a bleak evening. I turned to him, somewhat in despair at the thought of another week apart.

'I don't want to go home!' I cried.

Unexpectedly, Neil looked straight at me with an oddly serious look on his face. 'Marry me, then,' he said, deadpan.

The proposal was a surprise, and we left it at that, almost as a joke – but his words fogged in the cold air, like promises you could reach out and touch. And so I asked him about it a couple of days later when I rang him.

'Did you really mean that?' I said to him on the phone, the hope catching in my throat.

'Yeah,' he said, as matter-of-fact and down-to-earth as he always was.

I took a deep breath. 'The answer's yes,' I told him.

We went ring shopping the very next weekend. I was seventeen, which seems so young now, looking back, but I was sure about this man – and I have never been so sure of anything, before or since. He gave me a beautiful engagement ring, a pale-blue sapphire surrounded by diamonds, and for the rest of his time at Leeds we were engaged to be married. While Neil completed his degree, I finished my one-year YTS placement, and then did a two-year course in child development, just as I'd planned. We both graduated the same summer, in 1991, and spent four and a half weeks of the long holiday in France, living on a shoestring and a prayer.

Moving in together after the summer was an obvious next step. And it wasn't just a financial decision, or even necessarily to do with us as a couple, if I'm being completely honest. I came from quite a difficult background, you see, as my father was an alcoholic. He was depressed, and often suicidal. Neil was aware of everything that was going on at home, and he was in many ways my protector, taking me away from it all. Things were very, very tough at home at that time, and I knew Neil was keen to get me out of that situation. I had grown up with it, so I always thought of myself as tough and resilient, but he could see that the softer side of me was getting hurt. We both felt our own place would offer sanctuary not only to me, but also to my mother and little brother, should they need it. Moving out became a priority.

Neil had been sponsored through university by an electronics and software company and, as it happened, as well as offering him a job post-uni, they also offered him a relocation package, where they would cover many of the costs of buying a house. It would have been looking a gift horse in the mouth not to take them up on it. Neil's dad pitched in to help with the deposit, and my parents bought us a bed, and some friends of the family gave us a dining suite and two chairs. There was so much generosity that, in the end, the standing joke was that we moved into our house for the £15 it cost us to buy a second-hand fridge-freezer.

The house was a bay-fronted, three-bed semi in Leicester and it was a DIY dream – or nightmare. We moved in just before the Christmas of 1991, and the cold was like nothing I'd ever known. There was no heating, and the toilet was outside. We would have to sit in bed with a hairdryer, running it under the bedclothes to warm them up, and there would be ice on the inside of the windows. But it was home – it was *our* first home – and for that reason it will always be special.

Because family is really important to me, right from the off I was thinking, *I'll either have a baby or some cats …* As Neil put it: cats it was. Two ginger girl moggies, Meg and Tarragon – whom we nicknamed 'Taz cat' – joined us in our new home. They were sisters, but you'd never have known it to look at them; I think we got the largest and the smallest kittens from the litter. Meg was a skinny little thing, and Taz cat was huge. They were both almost feral when we got them – they were rescue cats – and they spent most of their time hiding beneath the telly. But one day, when I'd had some time off work from my job as a nursery nurse and had devoted it all to coaxing them out from their hiding place and giving them some love, I managed to persuade them to soften. Neil came home to find them both on my knee, and from that point on we were inseparable.

Both the cats were bonkers. I'd have to eat my breakfast in the middle of the room because, if I went anywhere near a counter or a wall, the cats would scale the surface and leap onto my shoulder to nestle there – and they wouldn't want to get off when the time came for me to go to work. Neil and I did loads of DIY in that house – knocking down walls, putting a bathroom into one of the bedrooms so we didn't have to use the outside loo and so on – and Meg would sit on my shoulder through it all; I'd literally be power-drilling holes in a brick wall with the drill in one hand and Meg on my drilling shoulder, like some kind of piratical parrot. They were a great team, too: Meg used to go out hunting huge moths, and she'd bring them indoors to show off to her sister, who would promptly eat the sacrificial offering and send Meg out for another. Taz cat was always eating. She got so large at one point that we had to buy a small dog flap for her to get in and out of the house. We put her on a diet, dry food only, but then she'd go off exploring and come in smelling of canned cat food, having charmed her way into some stranger's home.

Oh, they were wonderful cats! Dusty lived with Neil's parents, so the cats were our only pets, and all the more beloved for it.

In January 1993, a few months after my twenty-first birthday, my dad committed suicide. It wasn't unexpected, but it was still a shock. It meant that he wasn't around when, on 22 May 1994, Neil and I finally married. We had wanted a small wedding, but Dad had always been keen on a big family knees-up, and in the end we compromised and used some of his inheritance to stage the day he'd wanted for us. He had always said it was his dream to walk me down the aisle; it was my mum who did.

I saw a fortune-teller in the run-up to the wedding. She was based way up in Yorkshire and didn't know anything about us, yet she described my wedding dress to a tee – even though only Mum and I had seen it – and she also told me: 'Your dad will be there.' And so I still believe he was, to this day. As I walked down the aisle of the village church in Scraptoft, in my cream silk Ronald Joyce dress and ivory veil, watched by all the villagers, who'd crammed into the church till there was standing room only, I believe he was with me. I believe he was there as Neil and I exchanged our vows in the sunlit vestry, with Neil dressed in a handsome burgundy waistcoat and a dark morning suit. I believe he was there as we lit a candle just for him, after the ceremony. All the family were there, wishing us well. It was one of the happiest days of my life.

Neil and I always planned a large family; it was something we often used to talk about. Even though both of us had only one sibling each – Neil has an older sister – we wanted a bigger family than that for ourselves. I was sure I wanted an even number of children, and Neil began negotiating from a starting position of five kids, so four seemed a good compromise even before we got going …

Given these large-scale plans, it was perhaps just as well I fell pregnant when I did, in the autumn of 1996. It was an 'oopsie' pregnancy, as we later termed it (I was on the Pill and only just twenty-five, and babies weren't supposed to be on the agenda quite yet …), but from the moment we found out, we were both dead chuffed. I guess you can always sit there and say, 'We can't afford it, we haven't got time, it's not the *right* time …' so then that 'decision' was taken out of our hands, which was actually perfect. All three grandparents-to-be were thrilled, as this was to be the first grandchild for all of them.

During my pregnancy I used to lie on the sofa in the evening and Taz cat would lie heavily across my bump, like a warm ginger blanket. If the baby kicked, she would jump off and gaze quizzically at my bump. She would always climb back on, though. From the word go, we all felt a lot of love for the new little life growing inside me.

Our daughter, Lauren, was born on 13 August 1997. She was three weeks late, and it wasn't an easy birth by any means – I was induced, spent an entire day in theatre, endured a Ventouse not once but twice, as well as forceps – but after it was all over, when I held my newborn baby in my arms, I turned to Neil and said, 'I could do all that again.' (For the record, he looked at me with utter astonishment!) But she was worth it. She came out screaming her head off – and no wonder, after all that – but the moment they laid her on my chest and I said, 'Come on, Lauren, that's enough,' she just stopped crying. She was calm and went straight to sleep for 12 hours. You could almost hear her thinking, when I spoke, *I recognise that voice*, and then she nestled into me and dropped off.

I remember looking down at her as she lay peacefully in my arms, sleeping such a sound, sound sleep. She had a mop of jet-black hair and was just gorgeous. I remember telling her her name: Lauren Turner. We chose it because we thought it was a strong name. We'd envisaged it on a name plaque on an office door, and we thought – whoever she might become – that Lauren Turner sounded like someone who could take on the world, and win. That was my little girl, all 7lb 13oz of her.

I loved being a mum. I absolutely loved it, from the very start. As Neil had changed jobs to become a freelance software engineer in the airport industry – which basically doubled his income – I was lucky enough that after the birth I didn't have to go back to work, so my entire focus was on my baby. With my child-development background, I was aware of the usual milestones and Lauren hit them all dead on the dot, if not ahead of the curve. She was always smiling and giggling, and I used to talk to her all the time, as Taz cat curled around my legs, fascinated by the newest member of our family. Meg, sadly, wasn't around by then – tragically she'd been hit by a car when she was only a couple of years old – but Taz cat, in all her enormous girth, was an ever-reassuring presence for me as a new mum. She seemed to nod sagely at all I did, and was always available for a cuddle on the sofa after Lauren had gone to bed.

In the spring of Lauren's first year, I told our baby all about the new house we were moving to. Daddy and I had fallen in love with it, I told her animatedly, and I described the beautiful, four-bedroom, red-brick detached home that would soon be ours – and Taz cat's. We moved in on our fourth wedding anniversary. It was on the other side of Leicester, close to the biggest Marks & Spencer in Europe. (No wonder we had fallen in love with it!)

Lauren continued to flourish in our new home. She spoke early, and by eighteen months was speaking in fluid full sentences. She was very chatty – just like her mum – and extremely independent. It wasn't long before I had some more news for her: she would soon have a baby sibling to play with.

Joe was another 'oops', but another welcome surprise. He was born on 26 January 2000, when Lauren was two and a half. He was huge, a big biffer of a baby at 9lb 10oz, and, like Lauren when she was born, had a head full of thick dark hair. And he was hungry. Oh my, was he hungry! He ate all the time, and when he wasn't eating, he was screaming. To say he was hard work as a baby would be something of an understatement …

To be honest, though, I think he just wanted to move. Because, as soon as he hit three months and could roll to where he wanted to go, he was much happier – *and* quieter! A couple of weeks after accomplishing the roll, he was commando-crawling, and once he was up, he was off, and he was *happy*. He was a very active baby – he had been in the womb, too; he never stopped kicking and rolling – and one of his favourite pastimes was chasing the cat. Taz cat was pretty docile, so she endured all his attentions, even letting him tickle his face with the end of her tail as the pair of them curled up under a table together. Joe reached all his physical milestones super-quickly. Like Lauren, he spoke early too. It is with some amusement that I recall his first word, as it says a lot about me and my house-proud nature.

Not for Joe the likes of 'Mummy' or 'Daddy' or even 'Lauren'. Oh no! Joe's first word? 'Hoover.'

Lauren was a major part of his life, nonetheless. She was an ideal toddler, and had a nurturing nature from day one of her little brother's life. I could leave Joe on a playmat while I nipped upstairs to get something, and I'd come down and Lauren would be talking to him or singing to him – it was so sweet. She was such a caring child. I remember her nursery calling me in once to discuss a problem. Instinctively, I was worried – *What's she done …?* – but it turned out their concern was that, if someone snatched something from Lauren, she'd just say, 'It's OK, you can have it.' She had to be taught to make others wait their turn.

By the time Joe was born, Lauren's hair had become platinum blonde and curly – Joe's would later follow the same way – and she was the cutest little girl you can imagine. She learned to write and draw from a very young age and she would write little Post-It notes to us and stick them near our bedroom door: 'I love you Mummy' – things like that. We were a very affectionate family.

As Joe grew older, one thing I really noticed about him was his desire for eye contact. He used to pull my face – *anyone's* face – towards him to talk. I remember Neil's sister Helen saying, 'He always looks straight at you; it's almost as though he looks into your soul when he's talking to you.' Joe always had a need for cuddles too, almost a physical need. He'd be sitting in his pushchair and say, 'I need a hug,' and you'd have to give him a hug there and then and he would just melt. Then he'd say, 'I feel better now,' and carry on with his day.

The only cloud in our lives was that Neil's job in the airport industry meant that he often had to work away from home, and would be absent for long periods of time. As I had done the first summer we fell in love, I missed him like crazy whenever we were apart. And, no wonder, the children did too. All this came to a head in the summer of 2001, when Lauren, Joe and I walked past a factory one evening. There were no vehicles in the car park and Lauren turned to me in confusion and said, 'Where are all the workers?'

'They've gone home,' I replied.

'Why?' she said.

'That's what people do when work has finished,' I explained.

She looked up at me, her fiercely intelligent green eyes intensely puzzled. 'My daddy doesn't come home,' she said bluntly.

Well, how could we ignore that?

We started house-hunting for somewhere between Leicester, where the kids' grandparents lived, and Neil's work, which was based at Heathrow. Bicester was the answer, and we ambitiously took on a huge mortgage on a beautiful five-bedroom detached property. We moved in September 2001 and the future seemed rosy. But ten days later, due to the tragic events in America on 9/11, Neil lost his job.

It was a stressful time, to say the least. Aside from our shared horror and shock at what had taken place in the US, both the kids got chickenpox, Lauren missed out on a school place, we were financially under a lot of pressure, and every single day Neil was job-hunting without success. Having essentially lived apart for the past few years, we were also suddenly thrust into each other's pockets in a kind of hothouse situation, where all the stress was magnified. I went back to work for a bit to help out, doing a term of supply as a nursery nurse at a local school, and then more cover for them after that. In many ways, it was make-or-break for us as a family. But we made it. After six hard months, Neil managed to get another job and, slowly but surely, our fortunes started to improve again.

While we had struggled to get ourselves back on an even keel, our plans for a large brood of children had naturally taken a backseat. But as the Christmas of 2003 approached, I felt confident enough to broach it with Neil once again. As our little family of four sat around the dinner table one evening, Lauren and Joe chattering away happily to each other, I turned to Neil and said quietly, 'Do you think we can have another one?'

My husband's lovely green eyes rested on our two angelic-looking blond-haired kids; I didn't doubt that he couldn't help the smile that came easily to his face. He looked back at me with such love in his eyes.

'How can we say no?' he told me. 'How can we not want any more like that?'

I came off the Pill that same night. Two weeks later, Neil and I went to his office Christmas party, and two weeks after *that*, I found out I was pregnant.

Toby Turner was on his way.

2

Different

'You're looking positively blooming, Vikky!'

I laughed and rubbed my burgeoning belly, swollen with pregnancy. 'Well, thanks very much,' I said to the other mum at the school gates, accepting the compliment with a friendly smile, which she returned in kind. 'Three kids are certainly going to keep me busy, come October.'

As if in agreement, Toby shot out a foot and gave me a gentle kick. I loved playing with his kicking feet so I stroked my bump affectionately. He'd only recently started sticking his foot out; I would tickle it until it went back in, and then he'd stretch it out again and we'd do the whole little routine from the top.

My friend and I got chatting about other things as we waited for our children to emerge from the school – the weather, the upcoming school fete, everything and nothing. It was always so sociable at the school gates and everybody talked to everybody. For a chatterbox like me, it was a real highlight of the day.

I saw Lauren emerge from her class guided by a cover teacher, Pam, and gave her a wave. She'd settled in brilliantly after a shaky start as a youngster, when she'd been quite clingy, and was now flying high in Year Two. Both she and Joe were great readers – somewhat academic pupils even at their tender age – and I knew Joe, who was now attending the pre-school attached to Lauren's school, was just itching to join his sister in the main classes. He would start reception that coming September of 2004 and already I could tell he would take the whole thing in his stride.

I strolled over to collect Lauren, Joe running ahead of me as usual, sporty as ever, and yelling his head off, 'Lauren! Lauren! *Lauren*!' Pam looked up at our noisy approach and gave me a broad, genuine smile. She was a really warm woman, with dark curly hair and glasses, and was someone you immediately felt at ease with. All the staff at the school were nice – and I knew many of them as colleagues, as I was still doing the odd bit of supply cover for the school as a nursery nurse – but Pam was particularly lovely. The very first time I'd met her, earlier in the year, she'd showcased her generous nature, and I'd never forgotten it. One lunchtime Lauren had told me that she wasn't feeling very well and needed to go home; I'd replied that was fine but we'd need to walk because I didn't have the car. It was only a fifteen-minute stroll for us, but Pam had overheard and the first thing she said to us was, 'I'll drive you home.' I thought that was a very special thing for her to do, in her lunch hour, and I'd always found her a very giving lady. She always had time for everybody.

'Lauren! Lauren! *Lauren*!' Joe yelled again, at his typical ear-splitting volume, and both Pam and I burst out laughing at his exuberance. Ever since he had learned to talk, Joe had turned into something of a motor mouth. Very, very talkative, he never, ever shut up! He was very short, and very loud, and pretty much what you got with Joe was a mouth on legs. No wonder his family nickname was Gobby the Hobbit.

'Lauren! Lauren! *Lauren*!' he called again, and I guided the two of them slowly out of the playground, simultaneously shaking my head at Joe's chattiness and giving Pam a cheery wave goodbye, as Joe yakked nineteen to the dozen at Lauren, telling her all about his day. Lauren, to be honest, struggled to get a word in edgeways. I called time by asking each of them what they'd like to do with the weekend ahead.

'Swimming!'

'Soft play!'

'Safari park!'

'The zoo!'

The answers came thick and fast. I liked to keep the kids really active, giving them every opportunity I possibly could, and so our weekends and half-terms and holidays tended to be crammed with days out and themed activities and special events. It wasn't unheard of, during a holiday, for me to take the kids out every single day, so that come the Thursday of the half-term week, when I excitedly asked the children, 'What shall we do today?' they simply replied, 'Can we not just stay at home, please, Mum?' The three of us – along with Neil when his work schedule allowed – would spend hours visiting museums and libraries and local farms and more. It was part of what I loved about being a mum: showing them the world, letting them discover who they were through what they liked and what they could learn. I was determined that the new baby wouldn't slow us down one bit.

And he didn't. Toby was born on 14 October 2004 and he was a dream. I remember holding him for the first time, utterly adoring this new baby, and the midwife saying to me, almost in surprise, 'Gosh, you're on your third child and you still look like you're so in love!'

Frankly, I was. We joke now that Toby looked a bit like a chicken when he came out – he was late, and his skin hung off him in a scraggly way, as though he'd been a big baby but then lost a bit of weight towards the end; maybe because he was late and things weren't working quite so well – but I didn't really see it, skinny and wrinkled as he was. I just saw this beautiful baby with a scattering of rosy blond hair and a funny platinum white stripe down the middle of his head, made up of brighter hair than the rest.

I'd had a Caesarean, and I remember saying to the nurses, 'Can you please take all these tubes and drips off me so I can hold my baby?' There was an immediate bond there, straight after his birth, as there was with all my children. To me, it feels as though you somehow open up physically, somewhere in your heart, and hold your children there inside you, for ever after. It's lovely.

Toby was a brilliant baby. He ate well, slept well, smiled well – he was just straightforward. My schedule was full-on from the moment he arrived, smack bang in the middle of the first term of school. My day would consist of feeding Tobes, putting him in a sling, walking to school and dropping the other two off, walking back, feeding Tobes, changing him, walking back to the school to pick up Joe (who was doing part-time to ease him into big school), coming back, doing lunch, feeding Tobes, feeding the cat, going back to pick up Lauren ... That was pretty much all it was, day in and day out. Whenever the other two were at school or tucked up in bed, though, I would take the opportunity to enjoy a cuddle with Tobes. Those times are so precious, aren't they? You don't get them back again. I made the most of every second.

His siblings bonded marvellously with him; I couldn't fault them. There was no animosity, no jealousy – they would simply lie next to him on the floor or sit across from him in his bouncy chair and play with him for hours, making his favourite toy, a soft brown bear (called, imaginatively, Bear), entertain him from morning to night.

Toby hit his development milestones steady as a rock, one by one, and though he was a bit behind Lauren and Joe on reaching them, those two had been so relatively advanced that I didn't bat an eyelid. It didn't seem to me that Toby was slow, just that he was 'normal'. His language in particular was slower to come, and even once he'd mastered individual words, he took longer to get going with more complex language and full sentences. But Gobby the Hobbit spoke enough for us all, and we just thought Toby was taking his time, going at his own pace, and that was absolutely fine with us. Not everyone is the same; Toby was just different.

When Tobes was coming up to a year old, I started to go back to work, doing the odd bit of supply again at the local school, working in partnership with the nursery teacher with the 'rising fours' – three-year-old children who will turn four that school year, the year before they start in reception. It was hard work, but it was also really nice. I loved being part of a community and the friendships I made with my colleagues. And I loved working with all the children; there is nothing better than working with kids. As for my own children, Toby took to my return to work like a duck to water. He separated from me with no distress and was looked after by a childminder. The family home ran like clockwork.

But then it came time for Toby to be weaned – and the mechanism in our clockwork suddenly jammed, completely unexpectedly. He came off breastmilk and onto pureed food with no problems, but getting him onto solids was another matter entirely. With Lauren and Joe, we had used 'finger food', leaving their meal laid out for them on their high-chair table so they could feed themselves, and that had worked really well so we tried to do the same with Toby.

Big mistake.

My heart dropped to the very bottom of my feet the first time he cried out.

'Too hot!' he yelled.

I rushed over to him, guilt propelling me across the kitchen, and tried the food myself, worried I'd hurt him. But it was lukewarm at best.

'It's not hot,' I said to him in confusion. 'It's not hot. Try it again, Toby.'

But he cried out, 'It's burning, it's burning!'

I wondered if it was food allergies, and so I tried him on something else – but nothing seemed to work. Whatever we gave him, he would react the same way; this wasn't an allergy. The food would be too hot, too crunchy, too wet … always it was just 'too' much of something. Often when we gave him new foods, he physically gagged on them. He refused point-blank to eat anything crunchy or juicy – apples were a double-whammy no-go area – and even textured foods like mincemeat made him turn away from the proffered spoon. Whereas Lauren and Joe had happily fed themselves, pushing food into their mouths with little fists squishing in every last morsel, Toby refused to touch his food. He would never pick up his dinner himself and eat it; I always had to spoon things to him or cut the food up into little pieces and pass them to him. I became a master at diversionary tactics, reading a book to him while we were at the table or distracting him as best I could to ensure at least some food passed his lips. At every mealtime, I had to make sure I was sat next to him to be certain I was getting enough calories down him.

Nonetheless, despite my best efforts, and our pandering to his peculiar demands for extremely bland food, sometimes he would eat nothing.

Nothing at all.

We battled against him in those cases. As far as we could tell, he was just being a very fussy eater. We would know that, for example, he usually liked a ham sandwich, so we would give him the tiniest square of sandwich and say to him, 'If you just eat that, you can get down from the table. Just eat that, Toby.'

But he would stand off for a very, very long time, and refuse to give in. His little mouth would remain tightly closed and he would roughly shake his head from left to right, his whole body taut. It became a battle of wills – and we were losing.

He became thinner and thinner. It was distressing to witness, but I tried to think of my child-development training. I would murmur too brightly to reassure myself, over and over, 'No child will ever starve themselves. No child will ever starve themselves.'

But Toby Turner seemed determined to try.

Lauren and Joe had always been good eaters, so I hoped that Toby might follow their shining example as they sat at our kitchen table and dutifully ate the healthy meals I cooked for us all from scratch. But Toby didn't seem to take much notice of what they were doing. I thought maybe it was because of the age gap, because they were at school so much of the time, leaving him on his own. Whatever the reason, he paid no attention to what they did, and kept himself to himself. He didn't learn by example, as I'd hoped, but forged his own way.

And that independence and assertiveness soon made itself known in other ways, too. He developed his own way of walking, with an occasional 'flap' – an arm or a leg suddenly shooting out from nowhere (a bit like he'd done in the womb, I suppose), or a manic jumping up and down. It wasn't an aggressive thing, it was more like he had so much energy it had to be released somehow, and his flaps were the energy's escape route. When we were walking along a path, people would sometimes have to move out of the way because he'd flick and kick his leg out or wave his arms. Lauren often walked with him, holding his hand, and she'd say, in her grown-up, big-sisterly way, 'Toby, walk sensibly.'

He'd reply indignantly, 'I *am* walking sensibly!'

As Toby hit the terrible twos, we experienced for the first time the terror of a toddler tantrum. Luckily for us, Lauren and Joe had never had them – something we put down to their being able to talk so early, so they could tell us what they needed – but Toby was as stroppy as anything, and would rage and shout and stomp about. The white stripe of hair on his blond head would glow brighter when he was angry, so we called it his 'gremlin stripe'.

But he didn't like to be teased. We were a family who often affectionately poked fun at each other – we called Neil's middle-aged spread, for example, his 'burger' and teased him that he rivalled me in the big belly stakes (for, as 2007 went on, I fell pregnant with our fourth child and was growing bigger by the day). But Toby just didn't get it; any of it. The others might be teasing me for cleaning a lot or something like that, being affably sarcastic, and everyone would laugh except Toby. Instead, you could see a thoughtful look creep across his face as if to say, 'What does that mean?' I remember saying lightly to him once, 'You're a silly sausage,' and he looked at me aghast, as though I'd gone quite mad, and retorted crossly, 'No, I'm not!'

Challenging and peculiar though his behaviour sometimes was, we felt we were keeping on top of it. Neil and I discovered the benefits of 'time out', and Toby would regularly be sent to 'think about what he'd done' on the bottom step of the stairs. It could be for shouting huffily at his siblings, or for having a stand-off about his food, or for an outrageous temper tantrum. We would give him 'time out' for three minutes, and hoped – as it does for so many other children – that this would do the trick.

But when we went back to Toby on the stairs and said, 'OK, Tobes, your three minutes is up,' he'd reply, 'No, I want to stay here longer.'

Well, I'd never heard any child say that before!

We thought it was a battle of wills again, him trying to put himself in charge of the punishment, so we got a sand-timer and said, 'OK, if you want to stay for longer, you stay for another three minutes.' We felt it needed to be us, the parents, who were in charge of the time limits, not him.

As the new school year began, and Toby started at the Child First Nursery in September 2007, just before he turned three, we hoped that making some new friends his own age might encourage him to settle down – to eat sensibly and to become aware of the extremities of his own behaviour. Toby was a bright and engaged little boy, full of enthusiasm and clear intelligence, so all the signs were good that nursery could be the making of him. I taught him his numbers before he went, repeating them to him every time we went up and down the stairs, counting the steps, and it was clear he had a really good mind for figures. He'd even proudly show off his knowledge to visiting grandparents, and to his brother and sister.

Like many little boys, he also developed a fascination with the Disney film *Cars* around that time, and anything to do with the movie was a hit. He watched the film over and over and over, until everyone else in the family could quote it word for word, but Toby never got bored of the repetition; if anything, he seemed to find it comforting. He had all the die-cast toys, clothes and books too. Almost certainly every other little boy in the nursery shared his passion, so we were hopeful that it wouldn't be long before he came home chattering about a new friend, and we would hear reports from his teachers of how well he was getting on.

But it wasn't to be. I remember how awful I felt when one of the workers hugged him and commented on how skinny he was. 'You can feel all his bones,' she said, shocked. His reports mentioned how he never touched the hot dinner they provided, but I didn't worry too much about that; he only went for a short day, three times a week, and I could fill him up at home, using sandwiches and distraction techniques. Also, over the summer, he'd finally agreed to feed himself – when he ate, that was – which meant I didn't have to sit next to him and spoon him every mouthful when we ate our meals. It was progress, of sorts. Nonetheless, what really struck us from his time at nursery was that his peers obviously weren't helping us on the food front as we might have hoped.

In fact, as the weeks passed by, it became apparent that, actually, it was his peers with whom he had a problem. Reports came back that Toby was refusing to join in at circle time and story time. He snatched toys off the other children and didn't want to share. He wouldn't take part in group activities with the other kids and – as we had discovered at home – he actually seemed to enjoy the 'time out' punishment of standing on his own. Frequently he would ask to be left alone for longer than the allotted time, rather than return to an activity that other children perceived as a treat.

As any responsible parents would, we discussed all of this with Toby himself and talked through – for the umpteenth time – why sharing was important and other things like that. Toby would sit and listen with Taz cat on his lap, mindlessly stroking her ginger fur over and over. To be fair to him, he really hadn't had to face that situation at home: despite the pep talk to Lauren when she was in nursery, she and Joe usually let Toby have whichever toy he wanted to play with; or the older two would be playing a game together that Toby didn't want to join in. So this was the first time he'd encountered another child who didn't put him first, and in some ways his attitude could be understood; it was a learning curve for him. Bearing all of this in mind, I didn't think too much about it and instead just rolled up my sleeves and got on with it. I simply thought, *OK, he's going to be my challenging child. I've had two who aren't too challenging; perhaps Toby is just going to be one of those strong-willed kids.* My essential attitude was: 'We'll deal with it!' And that's what we tried to do.

In October 2007, for Toby's third birthday, we gave him a much-wanted *Cars* cake – and took him to a Thomas the Tank Engine-themed day out. As usual on the kids' birthdays, I think I was more excited than the children themselves at celebrating Toby's special day. I loved any excuse to rejoice in them and to give them a day to remember. The older children were now at the age where we could host parties for them, and Lauren and Joe had already each had a birthday party that year. They both had lots of little friends from school and everybody came; they got on really well with their schoolmates and it was lovely to see. Toby was still on the young side for that, as he'd only been at nursery for a few weeks and as yet hadn't made any friends, but the whole family came on the day out for him, which was great.

He seemed thrilled by all the mechanised rides and the big characters that populated the park. Partly because I was pregnant, I didn't go on any rides myself, but Toby pulled Neil across to one he had picked out specially, a children's roundabout ride with a little wooden car that would be perfect for Toby to drive; it suited his *Cars* obsession to a tee.

The vehicle was only big enough for Toby, but Neil gamely held his hand alongside the circular ride as our son beamed up at him with that lovely open smile he had at that innocent age, just three years old and all excited about the treat ahead.

The engine started up, making the whole ride thrum with motion and energy. And suddenly, Toby's face crumpled and he looked stricken with fear. He held out his arms to Neil to be lifted off – but it was too late, the ride started going round.

'Daddy!' he cried, tears already on his cheeks.

'Hold his hand, Neil!' I shouted, seeing his distress.

And, to his credit, Neil did. He held Toby's hand all the way round the roundabout, running alongside the ride and jumping over the metal motor every time he reached it. If Toby hadn't been so upset, it would actually have been very funny.

The ride came to an end, and Neil lifted Toby down. Our little boy was inconsolable.

After that incident, he refused to go on any more rides, or the swings, or a climbing frame, or any other roundabouts, and he avoided all parks like the plague. Something in the sensory motion of the ride had upset him so badly that he rejected that entire side of his childhood outright, there and then, right up until he was about seven years old.

It was as though he had trusted the world, and the world had let him down by moving unexpectedly – and he wasn't about to forgive it in a hurry.

And my poor son was about to find out that the world had a few more unpleasant surprises for him yet.

3

Friends Indeed

I had forgotten how much noise newborn babies can make. That winter, Toby was finding out for the very first time.

On 8 February 2008, our fourth and final child, Ollie, was born, completing the family of four that Neil and I had always longed for. He was a chunky little thing, the smallest of all my babies but perfectly formed, and he had lots of fuzzy blond hair, so it looked like an aura was gleaming around his head. Frankly, it could have been a halo – he was a really chilled-out, contented baby, and I was very lucky, given that I was also juggling all the other kids' needs at the same time.

I think if you'd asked Toby, though, a halo would definitely *not* have been what he had in mind when he thought of Ollie. As soon as we brought him home from the hospital, Toby refused to be in the same room as his new brother. He would walk out if we walked in holding Ollie. Even if Ollie was fast asleep, quiet as a mouse, Toby would make a sharp exit. It made it very difficult, because Neil and I would have to split ourselves between the two of them. Toby kept complaining that Ollie was 'too noisy' and, do you know, we thought, *Fair enough*. I mean, the crying of a newborn stresses anyone out, so we just thought it was winding him up and he couldn't cope.

So we tried to be understanding, and we did our best to help the two brothers bond. We encouraged Toby to push Ollie's bright-red pram when we went out for a family walk, and considered it a huge achievement when, in March, three-year-old Toby held his brother for the very first time. To mark the occasion, we took a photo: Toby, in a red Bob the Builder top (another of his obsessions), looked apprehensively at Ollie in his arms, who seemed completely – and typically – nonplussed by the whole affair. We hoped, as usual, that Toby would see how well Lauren and Joe took to their new brother and follow their lead in time, for they were once again amazing. Lauren was in her final year of primary school then; she had straight blonde hair cut into a neat bob (not dissimilar to how I wore mine, in fact, though I'm sure she wouldn't appreciate the comparison!), and looked every inch the competent and sensible girl that she was. Joe was growing up fast too; he was into cycling and science by then, and was still as chatty as ever.

With our family complete, it seemed like the perfect time for a special celebration, so in the spring of 2008, when Ollie was only about six weeks old, we jetted off on holiday to that mecca of childhood: Disney World in Florida, USA.

Lauren and Joe were pretty much bouncing off the walls with excitement. With Toby's *Cars* obsession still as strong as ever, we had imagined that he would be, too, but it turned out the Disney element of the holiday was the last thing on his mind.

'Mummy,' he kept saying to me, over and over, 'I'm worried about the plane.'

'It's perfectly safe, Tobes,' I would reply, trying to jolly him along.

'I can't get on the plane,' he told me, deadly serious. 'It's going to go too fast.'

He would not stop talking about the plane, in all the weeks leading up to the flight. We'd booked the holiday before his experience on the ride at his birthday, but we would never have anticipated this intense fear even after that event. He was incredibly anxious about getting on the plane, how fast it would go, what that would feel like, how noisy it would be … In the end, I think it was only because he was so small and we could carry him on and distract him while we did so that we managed it at all. He was tense and cross throughout the whole flight, and sat with his hands pressed against his ears, even though there wasn't any more noise than there is on a normal flight. We couldn't understand it.

We hoped he'd cheer up when we got into the theme park. And it really was fabulous – brightly coloured balloons and characters, brass bands, the screams of happy children from a multitude of imaginative events, all baking under the shining glare of the Florida sun. I handed out sunglasses to all the kids and Toby snatched his from me and glued them to his head. He was still in a strop … and he stayed in a strop. Even by Toby's standards, this was exceptional behaviour. We spent two days in the park, and I think he cried and wailed and railed and fumed most of the time. We'd hired a pushchair to help us get Ollie around, but in the end Toby commandeered it. He sat grumpily inside and pulled the hood of the chair right over his head and down to his knees, so all you could see was the bottom of his pale white legs sticking out.

You could still feel the tension and the anger emanating through the checked fabric of the chair, though.

We just thought he was having a massive temper tantrum, being a typical toddler.

What else could it be?

He'll grow out of it, we told ourselves. *He's just going through a phase.* We tried to ignore his strops and give the other children the holiday of a lifetime, but it was hard, and Toby was extremely demanding.

There were only two times he was happy in the whole trip. The first was when we breakfasted with life-size versions of the Pooh Bear characters – Toby gave big-eyed Eeyore an amazing hug; I think he thought he was real – and the second was when we bought him a new Tigger toy, a long, super-soft cuddly tiger who swiftly replaced Bear in his affections to become his favourite.

It could have been that Tigger reminded him of our Taz cat, who was still with us and who was such a chilled, laid-back cat that she was a firm favourite of all the children, including Toby. He would spend hours with her on his lap, calmly stroking her ginger fur with his fingers. She was a special cat to have attracted his attention, because Toby actually preferred dogs as far as I could tell. He didn't have much interaction with them – Dusty had passed away from old age long ago and none of our other family members had dogs – but every time we were out and about and saw a dog, Toby would be straight up to the hound to say hello and to give them a pat. We were forever having to say, 'You need to ask first …' because he was completely unaware of the potential dangers. All he saw was a potential friend. We'd given the other children the same warning, of course, because it's something all young children need to learn, but unlike his siblings, Toby never changed his behaviour. It didn't matter what type of dog it was. Big ones, small ones – Toby didn't care. We found it interesting the way he could store up information about the different breeds and rattle it off; he was like a little professor in many ways. But with everything else we had going on, we didn't even consider getting a dog of our own. For a start, I couldn't see Taz cat welcoming that new member of the family with open arms.

Sadly, though, not long after we got back from Florida, it turned out that Taz cat wouldn't be welcoming *anyone* anymore – not Toby when he got home from another difficult day at nursery; not Joe when he wanted a little face tickle with her tail; and not me, when all I wanted was a cuddle from my old girl after I'd got all the kids into bed and was having a much-needed sit-down in the evenings.

One afternoon in the late spring of 2007, when Neil was away with work in Germany, I walked into the kitchen to find Taz cat collapsed on the floor. She was seventeen years old, and I knew it was serious. I phoned the vet straight away and said, trying to keep it together, 'My cat's dying.' I knew the vet well, and she knew I had a new baby and three other kids and so, bless her, she just said, 'I'm coming over right now.'

I got all the kids together and put Ollie into Lauren's arms. 'Right, guys,' I said, trying to stay cheery for them, even as my voice wobbled, 'let's go, let's get out of here,' and I took them over to our neighbour's, who watched them for me as I dealt with the vet.

It wasn't good news. I phoned Neil in tears. He was about to get on a plane back home from Germany, so he was miles away. We'd both known how old she was, but neither of us had wanted to face it. Neil was in tears too. 'I'm so sorry I'm not there,' he choked out. 'I didn't want you to have to go through this on your own.'

'I don't know what to do …' I murmured. I felt bereft – Taz cat was more than just a family cat, she was the family heart.

The vet rushed her off to the surgery. We knew it was heart failure, and that her prospects didn't look good, but we hoped against hope that they could maybe give her some drugs and make her better. Meanwhile, I was beating myself up, thinking, *I should have acted sooner, I should have noticed there was something wrong …*

The call came at 10 p.m.

'Vikky?' our vet said. 'I'm so sorry. She's very badly brain-damaged. You're going to have to come.'

And so Neil and I made the decision, that evening, to have her put to sleep, to lay her to rest. I was absolutely heartbroken. Neil was the strong one who went to be with Taz cat in her final moments. She'd been with us through everything. I'd had her since I was twenty-one: before my dad had died, and all of that, through our wedding day, through all four children being born and growing up, through our struggles in 2001 and all of Toby's strops and scrapes … and now she was gone.

I don't show my feelings very often; I'm the type who battens down the hatches and weathers the storm. But I'd always been able to show them to Taz cat, if I wanted or needed to. She had always listened, and understood.

I couldn't believe I would never get to cuddle her again.

Waking up that morning was like waking up to a whole new world: everything felt different. I rolled over in bed and said to Neil, 'I can't not tell the children.' There was no way I could keep it from them, because I couldn't keep myself together. I remember telling them and the kids were as distraught as I was: she'd been around for *all* of their lives, and now she was no more. So we all had the day off and spent it together, grieving. We went to the garden centre and picked out a rose bush for her, one studded with beautiful pale-pink blooms. It was called Memories. The children drew pictures for her of times we had shared and we buried her with them, with the rose bush planted on top. Every single one of us cried. Even now, if you catch me in the wrong mood, or looking at that rose bush on a certain day at a certain time of year, I am still moved to tears.

For I had lost a friend, and I knew, even then, that she was irreplaceable.

And I was right.

The timing could not have been worse. For little did I know it then, but I was about to need friends more than I ever had before.

4

A Bad Reputation

'Come on then, kids, get a wriggle on, we don't want to be late for the first day of school!'

It was September 2008, and a new term was beginning in T-minus 30 minutes. There was a general scraping of chairs against the kitchen floor and a clattering of cutlery as Lauren and Joe finished their breakfasts and raced off to get their school things together. Only Toby stayed in the kitchen, shaking himself bizarrely. He wasn't having a flap; this was different. I looked at him in puzzlement.

'Come on, Tobes, we don't have time for this. Get a wriggle on!'

He looked at me angrily, still waving his limbs and bending his knees up and down, almost shimmying from side to side. 'I *am* getting a wriggle on!' he shouted, cross to be told off when in his mind he was doing exactly as I'd asked. I looked at him; he was right, he *was* wriggling, like a worm caught tight on a hook.

'No, I mean …' I trailed off. Why didn't he understand? I sighed, and changed tack. 'It's time to go. Go and get your bag for pre-school, sweetheart.'

He huffed off to his room, stomping up the stairs, and I watched him go with some trepidation. He'd been much better behaved over the summer, with fewer tantrums, seeming to enjoy the structured play and activities we'd done together as a family, and even to appreciate the little tricks that Neil and I had used with the kids since Lauren was small – like five-minute and two-minute warnings to the children before we changed what we were doing – but it appeared the honeymoon phase was over. With four kids, to be honest I *had* to be structured, but it had somehow suited Tobes to know exactly when lunch would be and exactly how many more minutes he had left to set up his Happy Street train track or to line up his Bob the Builder vehicles just so. I had noticed he never played imaginatively with them, but you could be sure that not a wheel was out of place – at least, not until seven-month-old Ollie crawled into the same play space and wrecked everything. Toby was still not a big fan of his little brother.

We'd only really had one massive meltdown, in fact. Holidaying in Chard with Grandma, we had all got ice creams and were happily licking them on the beach. Toby had started gasping because a wasp had landed on his 99, so I'd flicked at the creature with my hand. Unfortunately, both wasp and ice cream felt the blow and the vanilla scoop tumbled from its wafer cone and splattered on the floor. Toby, understandably, screamed his head off, but before we could promise to get him another or calm him down, he tore off along the beach, angrily stomping on the stones, which slipped and slid beneath his feet as though they were deliberately antagonising him.

As families do, we laughed gently at this drama-queen strop and watched him go. I knew he needed to let off steam and sometimes a good stomp on the beach is the best thing for that. *Any minute now*, I thought, watching him power-walk through his anger, *he'll turn around and come back. I'm sure he'll get to a point where he'll have had enough and he'll retrace his steps.*

But he kept on going. I raised a hand to shield my eyes from the sun and squinted. He hadn't looked back once. *Any minute now*, I thought, *he'll look round and see how far away he is from us and start coming back.* But he didn't. Not a single look; not a single sign he was bothered about leaving us behind. In the end, I'd had to go after him and persuade him to come back. Most children have a kind of safety mechanism that kicks in; it's the thing that, when they 'run away', makes them go no further than the end of the drive. But whatever it was, it seemed to be broken in Toby. And after that incident, he became a nightmare for running off. I had taken to dressing him in brightly coloured clothes all summer, luminous shades of yellow and orange and green, so that we could see him all the time. It almost didn't feel safe not to.

Watching him leave the kitchen now, small and huffy, he didn't seem anywhere near mature enough to be starting pre-school, but he was actually older than Lauren had been at the same milestone, as he was an October birthday and she was August. Comparing them in my mind's eye, they seemed worlds apart. But that wasn't to say Lauren seemed grown-up, not by a long shot. She was starting secondary school that morning, and I could hardly believe it.

She stood in the hallway now, her smart new uniform seeming too big for her narrow shoulders, and her new bag far too heavy for them, filled as it was with all kinds of stationery: pens and protractors and rubbers and set squares. And she looked anxious. She was the kind of girl who never liked to get things wrong, and to be transferring to a big school where she didn't know the rules was clearly worrying her. I gave her a big smile and a quick hug and wished her luck, as Toby and Joe barged around me and I gathered all three younger kids to take them off to the primary school (Neil was giving Lauren a lift). Our new cats, Charlie and Lola, stayed out of the hullabaloo; with Lola, a beautiful long-haired tabby, watching all the chaos disdainfully, as she did most things. The cats, nice as they were, were not a patch on Taz cat, and none of us seemed to have bonded as well. Toby in particular didn't hold much truck with them; they seemed too fast-moving and unpredictable for him.

The same could perhaps be said of the other pre-school children he met that morning. I was working in his classroom, assisting the teacher, so I had ample opportunity to see how he kept himself to himself, playing *alongside* his classmates, rather than *with* them. *Oh well*, I thought, *it's the first day. He's got all year to make friends*.

Yet as the term drew on, he still seemed awfully lonesome. I worked two days a week, so I wasn't there all of the time, but I saw enough simply from watching him in the playground. At break time, the other children would be engaged in playing games, playing really nicely together, but Toby would pretty much ignore them – unless they were playing with something he wanted. (And it was more like something he *needed*, actually; there was that intensity to his desire.) Then he would snatch it from them. I spent lots of time explaining why that was wrong, trying to get him to ask before he took things – 'Tobes, you need

to say, "When you've finished with that, please may I have it?"'
In the end, he would ask, but I got the feeling he was doing it
by rote, because I'd told him over and over to say it, and that the
concept of sharing was still as alien to him as a UFO.

To my sorrow, he started to get a reputation as a naughty boy.
Inside the classroom, at carpet time, he'd refuse to sit down. I'd
worked with enough 'rising fours' to know that some children
do find it difficult to follow the teacher's instructions and sit
still, so I just thought, *He'll learn*. And it was a learning curve
for me as much as him. Lauren and Joe had been so compliant –
I remembered them always being the first ones sitting on the
carpet, desperately wanting to please people – but it seemed
Toby didn't want to be a people-pleaser at all.

As the weeks went by, despite my hopes, he *didn't* learn.
Carpet time at school became like feeding time at home had
once been: a battle of wills. And when it came to such battles,
Toby had a fierce strength that belied his age. He would have
huge temper tantrums when the teacher asked him to behave
or to sit down nicely – to the point where they had to move
the other children away from him. I can still remember them
all staring at him with their eyes out on stalks as he flailed and
shouted.

He refused to come in from break time. It would be lining-
up time, and everybody would be filing up nicely, as obedient
as soldiers in a drill … all except for Toby, who would be off
down the playground somewhere, AWOL. It would take the
staff a long time to round him up. And it became a game –
for Toby. The teachers would be running after him and he'd be
running faster. It could have been he was simply trying to avoid

going in, because he came to really dislike going to pre-school. Sometimes he'd tell me he felt sick in the mornings, but once I ascertained there was nothing seriously wrong, I had to take him in.

His bad reputation soon reached the ears of other parents. One time, when I was standing in the playground that autumn, as Toby exuberantly raced against himself, I saw a mother dart across the concrete to her child. She spread out her arms as though defending her son from an armed gunman, shielding him as Toby ran past, though there were metres between them. Another time, Toby did bump into a child, completely accidentally, and I heard their mum run up and say, 'Are you OK? Are you sure you're all right? Was it *Toby*?' His very name seemed to take on a talismanic terror.

Nevertheless, for his birthday that year, we decided to hold a party for him and his classmates. His fourth birthday fell on a Tuesday, so we held the party at the weekend (which, as it turned out, was for the best, as he was very poorly on the actual day; physically sick as he opened his presents). We invited lots of people from pre-school. Though the mother who shielded her child sent me a cool email saying sniffily of her son, 'He *won't* be coming,' I was pleased that we did get lots of positive responses. Probably 20 children came, and we hired a magic man to entertain them. Toby had a great time. He was actually quite egocentric about it: he sat at the front of the audience and was part of it all. As I watched him sitting amongst his peers, I thought to myself, *Maybe this will be the turning point.*

A week or so later, it was the half-term holidays. The entire family seemed to breathe a sigh of relief. I knew Toby was delighted not to have to go in to school, but strangely enough, Lauren also seemed pleased (previously, she had always loved going to school, and the holidays had almost seemed an unwanted interruption to her education). When I mentioned this to her, though, she just shrugged it off nonchalantly. *My little girl's growing up*, I admitted to myself. She was normally really chatty, on any subject, but ever since she'd started at secondary school she'd become a lot more withdrawn and quiet; becoming a typical teenager, I'd guessed.

I could only hope she wasn't getting too old for our family outings. As usual, I'd planned an array of activities for us all that half-term holiday. We went to the cinema, which all of us but Toby seemed to enjoy (he sat with his thumb in his mouth, one hand over his ear and the shoulder of his thumb-hand pressed awkwardly against the other ear the whole time, as though the sound was deafening to him). And then I also scheduled in a day trip to the Longleat Safari Park.

I should have known it would be busy; it was half-term, after all. But it was *really* busy. I scanned the crowds nervously, thinking of Toby's habit of bolting. Every time I took him anywhere now, I found myself 'casing the joint', looking out for potential dangers and pitfalls. He seemed to have no sense of danger himself, so it was my responsibility to look out for him, just in case. I was always alert to where the busy roads were, or the nearest exit, or a steep drop down a hill. For when Toby ran off, he ran blinded by that intense energy and anger he had, as though his gremlin stripe had burned so brightly it had singed his sight, and I knew he didn't look where he was going; he was incapable of it when his tantrums took hold of him.

There didn't seem much chance of him running today, though: there was no space to do so. The crowds were so tightly packed we made very slow progress as we edged our way through the park. It was almost claustrophobic. Surrounded by strangers, I said clearly to Toby, 'You need to hold my hand.' I didn't want him disappearing; we would never find him again in the crush of people.

Ollie, meanwhile, was sitting perkily in his pushchair, craning to see the animals. He was a bright little boy. Like Lauren and Joe, he'd been ahead of the curve with his milestones, ever since he'd been born. In fact, his great progress had brought into focus how much slower Toby had been. Neil and I would think to ourselves, *Toby wasn't doing that at that age; he wasn't doing such-and-such either*. As with Joe before him, Ollie was very good at making eye contact with you, gripping your face with his little hands and peering deeply into your eyes. Toby had always been good at making eye contact with us, but it had been apparent at pre-school this half-term that he wasn't very good at making it with anyone else.

He definitely wasn't making eye contact with anyone at Longleat, I realised. Glaring would be more like it. He was glaring at the crowds, getting angry at the queues, and as I watched him, he roughly pulled his hand out of my tight grasp.

'Toby, you need to hold my hand, please,' I said again. 'There are too many people here; you'll get lost.'

He turned to face me. I couldn't actually see his eyes; as usual, they were shielded by his sunglasses. Ever since we'd given him a pair at Disney World, he wore them everywhere, even on cloudy days. It didn't bother me; we've always been quite free and easy with those things. If any of the kids wanted to go around dressed as a ballerina for six weeks, it would be fine – so a simple pair of sunglasses certainly wasn't an issue. They were a staple of Toby's wardrobe now. In fact, every time he approached a door to go outside, he would say to himself, 'Glasses,' and run off and get them. He never went anywhere without them. Recently, even though we were coming into the middle of autumn, it had got so that we couldn't even go outside unless he had them on: he would say the sunlight hurt his eyes.

Even though I couldn't see his eyes, however, I could *feel* them, boring into me.

'*No!*' he said crossly. 'I don't want to hold your hand!'

I reached out and took his hand again. 'I'm sorry,' I said, 'but because you keep running off on us, you have to hold my hand. We want you to be safe.'

He pulled and wriggled. 'I don't want to!'

We edged along with the crowd again, hundreds of people moving as one.

'*Toby* …' I said: a warning. But as with the idioms I used that Toby didn't get, he never seemed to appreciate a change in tone as a signal he could read. It was the same with hand gestures. If you crooked your finger at Toby and beckoned, he wouldn't come forward to meet you. He'd stare at you blankly, scratching his head. So he didn't react to my stern tone of voice. To him, I was just saying his name.

Toby sighed: a big huffy sigh that told me he was on the edge of a strop. Almost unconsciously, I tightened my grip on his hand.

In response, he pulled and tussled with extraordinary strength.

And, the next thing I knew, he was free. He wasted no time, but bowed his head and stuck out his elbows and ploughed through the crowd, running, running, running.

'*Toby!*' I shouted.

But it was too late. The crowd had swallowed him up. Neil and I looked frantically around us for a small boy in a bright-orange top, but he was nowhere to be seen. Then, after what felt like eternity:

'There!' shouted Neil.

Already some way distant, propelled on little legs that burrowed through the forest of strangers' limbs, was a flash of neon orange. We merely glimpsed it before it disappeared again from view.

'I'll go,' I said. 'You stay with the pushchair.'

And I dived into the crowd.

It's much easier for a small boy to run through a sea of people than it is for a grown woman. As I tried to push past, people tutted as though I was jumping the queue. Every part of my body seemed double size as I attempted to squeeze through the tiny gaps they left me. I was a tangle of awkward limbs and bum and belly, with no room to budge. 'Excuse me, excuse me,' I kept saying, hearing a tightness and a tone of panic in my voice, which was strangely high and unfamiliar. All the while I kept looking up ahead, trying to keep track of the orange flash. I wouldn't see it, and I'd feel an awful pang of dread in the pit of my stomach, and then I'd see it again and with renewed energy fight my way through the mass of people. *What if he gets out of the park? What if he goes off with a stranger? What if, what if, what if* … I couldn't stop the thoughts in my head. He was only just four; anything could happen to him.

'*Toby!*' I called out, hoping he'd hear and at least stop and wait for me. 'Toby Turner!'

There was nothing in response but more tutting and sighing. I elbowed my way through more rows of people and then, all at once, found myself in a little clearing. And there was Toby, up ahead, chest heaving a little from the exertion, looking grumpy and put out in his orange top and sunglasses, his head still bowed as though he would keep on running to the other side of the world.

'*Toby!*' I called again, and reached out an arm to still him.

He turned and looked back at me, and he didn't run.

I gripped his shoulders, fear making me hold him tighter than he probably liked. 'Toby,' I said again, trying to swallow down my alarm, 'you mustn't *ever* leave us. We need to be able to see you all the time. You need to hold Mummy's hand.'

He shrugged off my hands. The tantrum wasn't done. '*No!*' he shouted. 'I don't want to!'

I looked at him. He had no idea of the danger he could have been in; he never did. With a sigh, I reluctantly got a wrist strap out of my bag. It had two hand-holds on it: one for me and one for him. 'Well, in that case,' I said sadly, 'you'll have to wear this. If I can't trust you to stay with us and hold my hand, you need to wear this.'

I fastened the wrist strap on each of our hands. He was quite stroppy about it and really didn't like it at all.

To be honest, neither did I. Children are meant to fly free, not be chained to their parents. But if Toby couldn't be trusted to be responsible, it seemed our only option. Because he was not only putting himself in danger when he ran, but the other children, and Neil and me, too. I knew if he darted across a busy road I would be straight after him, traffic or no traffic. And what would I do if he ran when I had the other children with me – but no Neil to watch the pram?

As I turned and headed back towards the rest of the family – dragging a recalcitrant Toby with me, who lagged behind till the strap cut into both our wrists – I felt a shiver of foreboding. I couldn't really explain it. Toby was a difficult child, yes, but there wasn't anything *wrong* with him.

Was there?

5

This Isn't Right

New year, new family, I thought to myself that January of 2009, as we all headed back to school.

It had been a bit of a funny Christmas, all told. Toby had been poorly again, bless him. There'd been no warning sign of his being ill, but on 25 December, just as his siblings and grandparents and Neil and I were gearing up to come downstairs to see if Father Christmas had been, all of us whooping with excitement and saying, 'We're going to go downstairs and open presents!', Toby ran suddenly to the bathroom and was sick. He had to sit with a bowl beside him as he unwrapped his gifts. It was such a shame, particularly as I remembered his being poorly the year before, too; and he'd been struck with a virus on his birthday. The boy seemed to have no luck. Lauren was very quiet, as well, and I made a mental note to check in with her once things had settled down with Toby.

In general, my New Year's resolution started well, and Toby was thrilled in February to receive the 'Star of the Day' Award from pre-school. Without wishing to take anything away from him, in all honesty *every* child gets a turn to win it, so the fact he'd taken till February to receive it perhaps said more about his behaviour than gaining the award itself, but he was chuffed to bits and I was very proud of him too. *Maybe he's settling in now*, I thought, *maybe I've just been worrying too much*. After all, every mother does.

I still watched him closely in the playground, week after week. While most of the time he seemed happy on his own, sometimes I saw him watching the other children play. He always had a look of confused frustration on his face. You could see he just didn't get the games. They might be playing tag and he clearly didn't understand what was going on. To help him, I would say, 'Tobes, what you need to do is say, "Please can I play and what are you playing and how do you play?" Then they'll explain the rules to you and you can join in.'

Sometimes he'd try to join in anyway, without understanding, but that didn't always end well. There could be rough and tumble play between the boys and sometimes it went too far. Toby would get trapped and it would all kick off and he would get angry. Other times, I think he just felt enraged that he couldn't understand and so he would lash out and get in a grump.

All these attempts of his to join in came to a head one day that spring, when I received a phone call from the school.

'Vikky?' the teacher said. It was Toby's class teacher, Hannah. I knew her well, of course, because she and I worked closely together. She was a young woman in her late twenties with long blonde hair. We got on well, and would do things socially together, such as staff dos and the like, and there was a tradition that the staff would all go out for lunch together on a Friday afternoon; that sort of thing. She was good to work with and very organised, a kind of 'get the job done' sort of woman. But though we were friendly, it was unusual for her to call me during the day.

'Hannah?' I said immediately. 'Is everything all right?'

My first thought was of course that Toby had been hurt, and I felt my heart flutter.

'I'm afraid there's been an incident,' she said. And I'll never forget her next words. 'Toby's bitten another child.'

Oh no. I felt my heart sink, solid as a stone. I was gutted, absolutely gutted. I wondered if there was a reason for the biting, but from Hannah's account it sounded like Toby had simply gotten angry and hadn't known what else to do. It was almost like a defence mechanism as he tried to cope with the red rage in his head – not that I'm making excuses for him; what he did was downright wrong. Oh, it was just horrible. I was mortified. At the end of the day, you don't want your child to be *that* child, do you?

I went into school and picked him up and took him home to discipline him. I talked to him about what had happened, and even though I knew I shouldn't have done it, even though I knew this was not the way to go about it, I was desperate for him to see how wrong his actions were, and so I said to him sternly, 'If you bite someone else, I shall bite *you* and see how you like it!' But it didn't elicit much response. Like all my words of wisdom about sharing, and running off, and behaving at carpet time, the message didn't seem to sink in.

For that wasn't the only time he bit someone, to my shame. He did it on several occasions afterwards, and it always seemed to be the same children who got hurt. I remember writing letters to the parents of the students he'd bitten, apologising profusely and trying to explain, saying he finds it difficult to understand and, honestly, he's not a malicious child (and he really wasn't). I said, 'Please, if you have any problems, please come and talk to us and we can talk this all through.' They never did, though. And I got in trouble with my work for writing in the first place; it was all complicated, because of my being a staff member as well as a mum.

After the biting started, Toby and I were *personae non grata* in the playground. The parents would shun him and shun me too. It was so nasty sometimes. The overprotective parent (who now felt totally justified in her paranoia, I'm sure) would grab her child close to her if Toby so much as walked past. And I, too, found I was becoming more and more isolated; because the other parents thought it was my fault, I suppose. Bad parenting. It was just awful, so horrible. I had always been such a social person – I'll talk to anybody and I never judge – but now nobody wanted to pass so much as the time of day with me.

Being on my own much more than usual, I found myself watching Toby more and more often as the spring term went by, with a growing sense of apprehension. I would watch him when I was at work at the pre-school, and I would watch him when I dropped him off and picked him up. So many times, I saw him walking round the playground on his own with a big brown stick, just knocking it on lots of different things. He was always dressed in his bright-red coat that he wore with the hood up, with his ever-present sunglasses. And he just walked round and round and round the playground with that stick, banging it along the school railings.

Thuck, thuck, thuck, thuck … went the stick.

The other children ignored him, or shied away from him. But it didn't seem to bother Toby; not like it would have bothered me, or Joe, or Lauren, or even Ollie. As I watched him, one morning playtime in late March when I was on duty, after observing him for weeks, a thought struck me clearly for the very first time: *Toby doesn't* want *to make friends.*

Yet I knew from my child-development training that at that age children *do* want to make friends and they *do* want to play together.

In truth, I only had to look at every other child in the playground to know that.

Thuck, thuck, thuck, thuck …

As I watched him, I felt tears prick at my eyes. I would have felt emotional if I was witnessing someone else's child make his lonely way around that cold playground, but this isolated boy was *mine.* All the while I just kept thinking, *This poor child.* It was like he was in a different world to the other kids; that some invisible barrier kept him separate from them, not able to join in with their games. And it wasn't the biting, and it wasn't the carpet-time tantrums that had isolated him: it was something that had been there from the very beginning. Something inside him; something about my boy.

Thuck, thuck, thuck, thuck …

Another thought came to me, clear as truth: *he doesn't fit in.* Seeing him with his peers like this just made it totally apparent that he was different … and *how* different.

He just doesn't fit.

I blinked back the tears; I couldn't cry while I was at work. Yet I was reeling, feeling stunned. I felt like I'd been blinkered for years, and now these white truths were shining through, painful in their revelations and hurting me; just like Toby's eyes hurt when he didn't wear his sunglasses. The truth was too bright to look at, but I forced myself to – for Toby's sake.

Thuck, thuck, thuck, thuck …

Each bang of the stick revealed another truth.

Thuck … He doesn't interact with the other children.

Thuck … He doesn't understand relationships.

Thuck … He's so different to *all* the other kids.

Thuck … *This isn't right.*

The bell went for the end of playtime and, in a daze, I rounded up the children and we made our way inside. I tried to keep busy. I found it *really* hard to keep myself together, but I did my best. Despite myself, I kept seeing Toby in my mind's eye walking round and round that playground, over and over again … and always alone.

Somehow, I got through the late-morning session working on auto-pilot. When lunchtime came, Hannah and I went and ate our food together as usual in the staffroom. It was a large, noisy room with chairs placed all the way round the outside, and I tucked myself into a corner with Hannah beside me. We balanced our Tupperware boxes on our knees and for a moment there was silence between us, the hubbub of the other staff eating and chatting washing over us. I couldn't stop thinking about Toby.

Suddenly, I found it hard to eat my lunch; the food tasted like cardboard in my mouth. No longer hungry, I popped the lid back on my box and glanced sideways at Hannah, at my son's classroom teacher. I knew what I had to do, but doing the right thing had never seemed so hard.

I took a deep breath and felt the words I had to say on my tongue, like cold hard pebbles in my mouth.

'Hannah,' I began.

She looked up at me, and I knew I had to continue.

'I think there's something wrong with Tobes, isn't there?'

She smiled at me gently – but also with a kind of relief, I realised.

'I'm so pleased you said that,' she said frankly. 'I'm so pleased you came to me and said something.'

A part of me hoped wistfully that she meant she was pleased because there was nothing wrong at all and now she could dismiss my fears right away. But she hadn't finished. Instead of airily waving away my concerns, she said softly, 'I was just thinking that I was going to have to approach you.

'I think you're right. I think Toby has a problem.'

6

Taking Action

The air whooshed out of me in a sigh. That was hard to hear, even though I was the one who'd raised the issue in the first place. Perhaps I looked as though I might wobble and break down, right there in the middle of the staffroom, because Hannah stood up abruptly, reached out a hand and pulled me up.

'Come on,' she told me briskly, in her no-nonsense, let's-get-things-done kind of way. 'Let's go and find somewhere to talk.'

We went to her classroom and she immediately pulled some paperwork from a file. It was a two-page questionnaire: 'Early Years Action' read the heading, and then it listed all the different ways a child might learn and perform and interact. Hannah sat down next to me and together we went through each item on the list.

Did Toby 'not follow the usual developmental patterns'? *Tick*.

Did he 'find it challenging to learn and be part of small groups/class group/unstructured activities'? *Tick*.

Could he be 'easily frustrated and over-anxious'? I wanted to double-tick that one, but Hannah simply marked the box with a single black *tick*.

On and on the list went. Did he 'interpret language in a literal way', 'like routines to be the same', 'show sensitivity to noise and light', have difficulty 'forming relationships' and demonstrate 'disruptive behaviour requiring adult intervention'? *Tick, tick, tick, tick, tick.*

It wasn't so much a sinking feeling I experienced as we completed the questionnaire, it was more that every black tick just *hurt*. Fifteen minutes was all it took to answer the questions, but in those minutes I went from *thinking* there was a problem to *knowing* it. And even though I'd been watching him and silently worrying for weeks, the act of formally completing this questionnaire made everything horribly real. The world somehow tilted on its axis, as in a sci-fi story, for with every tick the future I'd imagined for my son vanished. Each stroke of Hannah's pen put a line through yet another dream I'd had for him and crossed it out, indelibly.

When you hold your baby in your arms, the very first day they're born, it's like a string is cast into the future and you can follow it along; like climbers do with tethered safety ropes on mountains. No matter what, no matter how they turn out, you know this child is going to grow up and become an adult and they're going to get a job and they're going to move out, eventually, way off in the future … But all of a sudden all that certainty just went. Now, everything was unsure; the future concealed within an opaque mist. I had no idea what Toby's future held for him now. Would he be able to live on his own? Have a career? These were suddenly unanswerable questions.

What I did know, though, was that he wasn't going to find it easy to make friends. He wasn't going to understand the world around him. Already he was struggling, but it was only going to get harder for him as he grew. *My son is going to find life really difficult*, I thought. I was just so sad for him; really, really sad. Life was going to be tough for little Toby Turner, and no parent wants that for their child.

I felt another emotion, too, as Hannah ticked her boxes and each one confirmed there was something wrong: guilt. For I couldn't help but think of every time Toby and I had faced off about his behaviour – when I'd battled with him to eat meals that he said were too hot or too crunchy but to me were just normal; when I'd sent him for 'time out' for unacceptable behaviour; when I'd told him over and over how badly he had behaved and that he had to do better, try harder … when, all along, he really couldn't help it. I had thought he was simply a challenging child, one who needed stepping on and sorting out to help him find his way in the world; that I'd needed to be the one to win our battles because, if I hadn't, *he* would have been in charge and you can't let children rule the world.

Memories flooded through me and I felt hot. The way we'd made him get on the plane to Disney World, even though he'd protested about the noise and the movement. Disney World itself, with its cacophonous brass bands and screaming children and the glaring Florida sun and brightly coloured characters. It must have been torture for him. I regretted all of it, every single thing I'd ever done when I hadn't understood him properly. I thought sadly, *I could have done it all so much better* … But it was too late now. I couldn't turn back the clock.

On the bottom of the form was an instruction: 'file with SEN action record'. I knew what SEN stood for: Special Educational

Needs. That was what my son had. We didn't yet have a precise label for him – though in truth I immediately thought of autism, from what very little I knew of it – but we now knew he needed help.

Hannah and I didn't discuss what the form showed us; there were so many positive indicators for SEN it was clear to us both that our suspicions had been right. And so, together, we then went to see the school's Special Educational Needs Coordinator (SENCO), who was none other than Pam, the kind cover teacher who had been so lovely when Lauren was poorly in Year Two a few years before. I was so pleased it was her. As always, she was warm and friendly, and her manner didn't change as Hannah talked her through the form. In fact, she nodded her head sagely in recognition, her dark curls bouncing, and turned to give me an encouraging smile.

'Right,' she said firmly, seizing the initiative. 'You need to come in and see me for a talk – and you need to bring Neil in too.'

Neil. What would he think of all this? I felt wobbly all over again, and very tearful. 'OK,' I said, taking deep gulps of air to try to calm myself down, 'I'll bring Neil in.' I spoke with tears glittering in my eyes, and I blinked them back again, trying to smile through the hurt.

On my way home though, later that day, the upcoming meeting with Pam – which was scheduled for the very next day – gave me a clear focus: something to prepare for, something to do. I have always felt that children are given to their parents for a reason; that your kids are specifically paired with you because you're meant to be together and you as a parent are meant to raise that particular child. As a consequence, I felt strongly that for some reason somebody had thought Toby was a good match for me. So I didn't feel sorry for myself as my mind ticked over what had happened that afternoon; I didn't ask, 'Why me?' or 'Why him?' Instead I asked: 'What can I do now to *help* him?'

The first thing I needed to do was bring Neil into this situation and tell him all that I'd discovered: Toby would need his father as well as his mother to help him through the challenges ahead. And so, as I drove the short distance back to our house, I got my organised head on. I was determined that I wouldn't let my emotions get in the way. If I got upset now, I felt I wouldn't be able to get my point across to Neil and emphasise the seriousness of the situation. Toby needed me to be strong for him.

We need to sort this out now, I thought to myself as I drove. *We need to help Toby as much as we can. We're going to get to the bottom of it and, if Toby needs extra support, we will get it for him right away.*

He is four years old now and he has been without it long enough.

Neil was at home when I got there. He was working from home a lot at that time, with trips away only once a month or so, and only ever for a few days: a change in the contract position at work had allowed such a schedule and it was an opportunity we had grabbed with both hands. It was about five o'clock in the evening, just before I needed to start making the home-cooked tea I prepared every night for the family. The kids were off in their bedrooms or in the playroom, so we had the kitchen to ourselves. It was now or never.

'Neil, love,' I said. He was standing near the kettle and looked round at me, perhaps sensing the determination in my voice. 'Toby's got some problems,' I began, 'we need to go into the school tomorrow afternoon and talk to Pam, the SENCO.'

Neil's eyes bugged out as he looked at me: a caricature of surprise. This was the first he'd heard of it. For, as was always my way, I hadn't breathed a word to him about my concerns about Toby; about how I'd been observing him for weeks, noting all the little signs that were telling me something was wrong. What can I say? I hadn't wanted to worry him with it. After all, what would have been the point? I'd been hoping against hope that the 'problem' I was seeing wasn't a problem at all, and I didn't want to worry him unduly. But the time for staying silent was now past.

For Neil, though, all this was coming out of the blue; he hadn't been festering over all the signs like I had.

'What are you talking about?' he said now. 'Toby doesn't have a problem.'

I could see why he would think that. Neil didn't have the front-row seat that I did at Toby's pre-school. He only ever saw him at home, in our well-structured household, where Toby knew exactly what was happening and when and why, and happily followed his routine. At home he was very well managed, and it was also apparent that he was extremely bright. Toby was like a little professor in many ways, holding forth on his favourite topics, about which he would become obsessed. He was so clever that he would even correct us adults if we happened to mispronounce a word, and he was full of obscure facts that stunned the grown-ups with whom he interacted. The idea of him needing 'special educational help' – with its implications of assisting someone slow and backward – jarred completely with the smart little boy Neil knew and loved.

'He doesn't fit in with the other children, Neil,' I said.

'Nah, he's fine,' Neil insisted, 'he's just independent.'

'Neil, seriously, he's got a problem. Hannah and I did this questionnaire and he scored really highly …'

But Neil was shaking his head, unconvinced. 'Nah …'

'Neil, he has a problem. We have a meeting tomorrow with Pam to discuss it. OK?'

'OK, Vikky …' he agreed, but I could tell he still didn't believe me. In fact, I think he thought we'd have the meeting and everyone would agree at the end of it there simply wasn't a problem. But that wasn't the way it turned out.

It must have been scary for Neil; I can see that now. While I'd had weeks to build up to my acceptance that something was wrong, each sign a brick in the wall of this new house I found myself living in, Neil had had it land on him overnight, like Dorothy's house in *The Wizard of Oz*. With the meeting happening less than 24 hours after I'd first raised it with him, no wonder he looked a little like a tornado had whirled through his life as we made our way into Pam's classroom the following afternoon.

Pam, at least, grasped the situation straight away. Despite my best intentions to be unemotional and strong for Toby, I couldn't help being a little upset as I walked in, and she immediately got up from the table and gave me a hug. With her arm still round me, she apprised my husband.

'Neil,' she said, 'don't look so frightened. It's fine.' She gave him a hug then too. 'Come on, let's just get this sorted.'

And so we sat in Pam's classroom, at those teeny tiny tables they have in primary schools, and Pam and Neil and Hannah and

I talked about Toby. We went through the checklist again and I could see the evidence stacking up for Neil as the professionals talked about our son. I could see him thinking, *They're right about Toby and something is going to have to be done*. From then on he was fully on-board, 100 per cent supportive of anything that needed to be done to help Toby.

At that point, Hannah and Pam couldn't say what they thought he had – and, in fact, a formal diagnosis of autism can take years to achieve – they were simply assessing his problems and trying to solve them for him. Luckily, Pam is just tremendous at her job. She puts in so much time and effort. Working together, we drew up an IEP (Individual Education Plan) for Toby, and this was when Neil and I discovered something new about our son.

'The thing I think we really need to focus on,' said Hannah, 'is Toby's self-esteem. He doesn't think he can do anything.'

I could feel Neil start next to me. This didn't gel with the boy we knew from home. But it was almost like Toby was two completely different children. At home he was well managed and calm and happy and confident; at pre-school he was anxious and insecure and fraught. His self-confidence wasn't something Toby himself ever talked to us about – he never said to us he felt he couldn't do things – but at school it was something he frequently shouted: '*I can't do it!*', followed by a glum spiral into self-disgust. Hannah wanted us all to help Toby feel more secure in himself, and Neil and I were completely supportive, even as we were sad that this was something our little boy needed.

Following the meeting, I slotted straight into 'let's get this sorted' mode. I went home and googled *everything*; reading, it was obvious to me that Toby was a high-functioning autistic child. I ordered a huge stack of books, all about how to help your autistic child at school – I think I've probably read every book about high-functioning autism that's ever been written. The best way to help Toby was to be as informed as I possibly could be about his condition, I felt, so I devoured every scrap of information and every suggestion and idea that I could possibly find. I simply felt it was my job as his mum to help him as best I could.

From then on I became a whirling dervish of activity, putting suggestions from both the school and the books into place. I made an 'I can' book for Toby, where we went round with him and took a photo of all the things he was successful at – tying his shoelaces, dressing himself, and so on. I remember we took a picture of him on the beach with some people sitting close to him; that was labelled 'I can play in the sand with friends'. Any opportunity we found where he was doing something positive, we would take a picture and praise him. The book was intended as a distraction technique, so that, when Toby was having one of those moments in school when he couldn't do something – sit on the carpet, line up, join in – and everything was going a bit pear-shaped and he was feeling really bad, he could look through the book and his teacher or I could say, 'Actually, look at what you *can* do.'

Very soon after my meeting with Pam, I called a lunchtime meeting of all the staff. Consistency is key, so I felt it was really important that every staff member understood what was happening and the measures we were putting in place to help Toby. I made up this marble reward scheme for him, whereby the staff could give him laminated pictures of marbles every time he did something well, such as sharing a toy nicely or coming in quietly after break. Neil and I would then transform the pictures into real marbles, and once Toby's marble jar was full, he would receive a reward (something *Cars* related, no doubt, with which he was *still* obsessed!). It was so important that my colleagues understood all this, so that Toby's good behaviour could be consistently rewarded.

To the same end, I made Toby some handouts to carry with him for the dinner ladies and other people he encountered, which introduced his difficulties and explained to the adults how best to help, just so they could 'get' him a little more. I always felt if people could understand him and make him feel safe then he wouldn't feel the need to kick off or to run away.

Hi, my name is Toby Turner, the handout read, followed by a picture of our smiley, green-eyed, blond-haired boy. *I have a few things to tell you to help you understand me better. I am a little sensitive to loud noise and bright light; I really feel the need to wear my sunglasses when I go outside.*

I tend to think in a literal way and things are very black and white to me, so if you tell me to get a 'wriggle on', I can wriggle really well.

I like my routine and if it gets changed without warning I can get a bit upset. If you explain to me beforehand I find it much easier. Also, two-minute warnings work very well when you need me to do something (come inside or share a toy).

I can become emotional because of the way I think. I sometimes understand things differently to you. I normally calm down on my own with a little space.

*Finally, if I make a good choice you can give me a marble
as a reward. Ask me, I'll show you how.*

Of course, pulling together these strategies – making the book,
writing the handout, laminating lots and lots and lots of pictures
of marbles – took up a great deal of time. I stayed up very late at
night, beavering away on the computer and snipping away with
the craft scissors, desperately trying my hardest to make things
right for Toby. Neil and I made the decision not to discuss his
'diagnosis' with him, partly because we still didn't have one, not
formally, but also because we wanted to focus only on building
him up and making him feel confident.

In some ways it was brilliant, my working at his pre-school,
because I could keep half an eye on him in the classroom and I
was always really quick to give him as much time and attention
as I could, but I was also aware of the demands of the other
children and how difficult it was for Hannah. When you're a
class teacher and altogether you've got 30 three-year-olds to look
after, that's really hard going, isn't it? I do think she found it very
difficult at times – well, as did I – because of the way he was,
because he was really hard work when things didn't go well. I
found I spent a lot of time with him straight after school too,
trying to smooth over the upsets of the school day, while the
other children settled around us at home. All the while I was
conscious of Lauren quietly sloping off upstairs to her bedroom,
of Ollie gurgling away to himself as he built tower blocks on
his own on his playmat, of Joe throwing himself on the sofa to
watch kids' TV, but Toby seemed to absorb my attention like a
sponge.

And then, one day, in the midst of all this concern and effort for Toby, we got a phone call from another parent at Lauren's school.

'Mrs Turner?' she said. 'I just wanted to ring to let you know my child witnessed Lauren being very badly bullied today. They were very distressed by what they saw so they told me all about it and, well, I just thought I ought to ring …'

I felt shell-shocked. My Lauren, bullied? Why hadn't she said anything? We were so close …

But then I realised: *when* would she have said anything? When she got in from school, my time was taken up by Toby. And when Toby was in bed, I'd been busy making books and handouts and marble pictures for him. I hadn't had time for her.

I felt like the worst mother in the world.

7

Dark Days

When Neil and I asked Lauren about the bullying, she broke down in tears. She hadn't told anyone about it and I think she was overwhelmed that the truth was finally coming out. Later, she would say how grateful she was to the child who spoke up, who'd been distressed at seeing her bullied. She said she never would have spoken out herself, despite the effect it was having on her: she was just too scared.

Lauren needed us a lot, after that. She'd been so brave for so many months, coping not only with the bullying but also the overwhelming feeling of being a small eleven-year-old in a big school with hurly-burly teenagers. She'd been very good at hiding how upset she was, but she didn't need to do that anymore. Neil and I rode into battle for her. I went into her school and talked to the welfare managers – the school was excellent: the bully was ultimately excluded – we both arranged a course of counselling for her through our GP, and Neil was indescribably brilliant. Now the truth was out, Lauren would sob all the way to school, every single morning, and her dad was the one who coached her to be strong and to survive. I'd have been tempted to turn the car around, wrap her in a duvet and force-feed her hot chocolate for the rest of the day, but Neil made sure she was always able to get out of the car. It may have been on shaky legs, but she would have a smile on her face and her shoulders back, ready to face the day ahead – whatever it held.

The thing that hurt the most was seeing how much pain she was in and knowing that I'd let her down. I'd always encouraged my children to come to me with problems – I used to say, 'I might not be able to make it better but I can always help you in some way' – but Lauren hadn't said a word to me. Only later (years later, when we were writing this book) would she confess that she'd felt guilty about taking me away from Toby, because in her mind, her problems were never going to be as big as his, and that's why she hadn't said anything. At the time, I didn't know that, and so I just felt hurt and guilty myself that I hadn't been there for her.

Toby still needed me immediately after school, but we made sure Lauren had our full attention after the boys had gone to bed. She used to spend a lot of time in her bedroom while her brothers were awake, but once they were tucked up asleep the three of us would come downstairs together and have a cup of tea and we'd talk then, snuggled on the sofa or sitting on Lauren's bed, with its pink flowery quilt. Sometimes, Neil and I would be in bed, the lights off and the house quiet, and Lauren would come to the side of our bed in tears, and we'd get her in with us and talk then, too. That would happen quite a lot. She was having a very, very tough time.

And she wasn't alone. Despite our new knowledge of Toby's condition, and my best efforts to put measures in place to help him, he was really struggling at pre-school. Some days, I'd go in to pick him up and they'd tell me he'd spent the whole session in the cloakroom and didn't go into the main class at all. I'd have to go and find him and he'd still be skulking in the toilets, really agitated and stressed, cross and upset, pacing like a cornered animal in the loos.

'Toby,' I would say. 'It's OK, Mummy's here now.'

At that point, we would just hug and cuddle, and then come home. We'd make a point of 'leaving school behind us'. We'd be standing hand in hand by the school gate, and we'd make a deliberate show of stepping over the threshold and I'd say to him cheerily, 'School's behind us, let's go home.' And as we left the school the implication would be that we were leaving that day's upset behind us too, whether it was a tantrum, or a teacher shouting at him, or his perceived 'failure' at some aspect of life or another.

Later, Neil and I would chat with him around the kitchen table, trying to understand. 'Why were you in the loos, Tobes?' we would ask him. 'What happened?'

He would always come up with things like, 'It was too noisy' or 'It was too busy'.

'Well,' I'd say, 'why didn't you play outside for a little bit? It can be quieter outside?'

But Toby would insist, 'It was too sunny' or 'It was too hot'. Everything was 'too' – too this, too that. His autism meant he was super-sensitive to any sensory stimulation. For him an echoing school classroom with 30 children's voices was like the seventh circle of hell. No wonder he hid out in the relative peace of the toilets.

Yet we soon found out there was another dimension to his self-enforced isolation – one that took my breath away. Whenever I worked a full-length day at the pre-school, Neil would pick up Toby, and he was on parental duty on this particular day; a day that had seen another biting incident take place. As I came home from school, a few hours after the boys, I discovered a peculiar thing on our upstairs landing. Along the walls we had photographs of all the children, an individual portrait of each beaming child, all of them blond-haired and smiling. They always made me smile in return, and I enjoyed the walk I made when I came home, up the stairs and along the landing to my bedroom. There was Lauren and Joe and Ollie and … *Oh!*

'Neil?' I called out. He was downstairs in the kitchen. 'Neil, what's happened to the pictures? To Toby's picture?'

He stuck his head out of the kitchen. 'I don't know, love.' He came upstairs and stared at the wall alongside me.

For Toby's picture had been deliberately turned around to face the wall. Just the cardboard backing showed where normally his lovely face would be, beaming out at us.

I went along the landing and knocked on Toby's door. As so often was the case, he was sitting inside by himself, his back against the bunkbeds. He had boxes of Lego and *Cars* and Bob the Builder toys to play with, and bookshelves full of books to read, but that afternoon he was doing nothing but sitting curled up in a ball.

'Toby?' I said gently. 'Toby, have you turned your picture around?'

He didn't say anything at first, but then he nodded: a definite dip of his small blond head.

'Yes,' he said quietly. 'I don't belong in this family anymore. I don't deserve to be here.'

My heart felt like it was breaking. 'You're *always* in this family, Toby,' I told him firmly. 'We *love* you. You must never doubt that, no matter what happens or what you do or anything, we will always love you.'

But he just shook his head. 'I don't belong in this family because I'm horrible,' he replied.

'You're *not* horrible, Toby.' I tried to reassure him. 'What happened today wasn't good, but it doesn't mean you're a horrible person.'

He shook his head again. 'I *am* a bad person!' he said, with that stubborn forthrightness that I knew so well. To him, it was an incontrovertible truth. Black is black and white is white, and Toby is a bad, bad boy.

'What makes you think that, Tobes?' I asked gently. I sensed there was a reason.

'Because they move the other children away from me,' he told me. 'When I don't sit down at carpet time and get angry, they move the other children. That's because I'm dangerous and a bad person. The other children aren't allowed to go near me.'

With every word, my heart was splintering. 'That's not why,' I said. 'That's not why, Tobes. That's *never* been why.' I thought back – they'd been moving the children away from his temper tantrums since the very first week of pre-school, way back in September. Had he been thinking these thoughts all this time? *Poor, poor boy.* 'They moved the children away so you could have a bit of peace and quiet to calm down. That's all, Toby. That's the only reason.'

'No,' he insisted. 'They moved the children because I'm *bad*.'

Nothing I said seemed to get through to him. Neil and I turned his picture the right way round again, but after that, again and again, we'd find it facing the wall whenever a day had gone badly. It didn't even have to be a serious incident like the biting. If Toby felt like a failure, which he did almost every day, his picture would be made to turn away, to signify his exclusion from the family, his sense of not belonging – of not deserving to be there. He took any cross words to heart. If I said, 'Toby, please don't play with that car' – perhaps because it was one of Ollie's and he'd snatched it from him – he'd reply, 'I'm never going to play with another car again for the rest of my life.' Everything was extremes with him, from his negative reactions all the way through to the affection he gave us. A hug from Toby had so much love in it that it would almost take your breath away as he squeezed you tight.

It was hard not to show him how his words and behaviour made me ache inside, but somehow I found hidden reserves of strength I didn't even know I had and – in front of him, at least – I was never anything but confident, reassuring and bright. I was like that in front of all the children, and my mum, and even Neil. I would share with Neil what I needed to share, what he needed to know, but the rest I just didn't talk about. I felt I had to be strong to hold the family together; if I showed I could not cope, it would all fall apart. Far better to say nothing.

The school year dragged on – and that's exactly how it felt, like it was dragging, pulling us all through the dirt to the bitter end. I think it was one of the hardest years of my life, what with Toby's struggles and our realisation that he needed help, and

Lauren's bullying and counselling, and Ollie being weaned and Taz cat having died the previous spring. I longed for the summer holidays like a plant longs for water. We just needed to get to the end of the summer term and then we'd all be free.

But the year had another sting in its tail before it was through – one I could never have seen coming in a million years.

It happened one afternoon, in May or June time, as I was driving to my mum's house with all the kids in the car. As usual, I was being bright and breezy, jollying them along, but perhaps something about my demeanour struck Toby as false. It had been a tough week – *every* week was tough around that time – and I'd spent hours with him after school, calming him down and trying to cheer him up after another struggle at pre-school. Even so, what he said to me in the car as I drove along came out of nowhere, and perhaps that's what made it worse, because he'd been thinking about it and storing it up, and it wasn't said in anger or in the heat of the moment.

'Mummy …' Toby said to me, almost thoughtfully, from his car seat in the back. He was still only four years old, but there was often a strange maturity in the way he expressed himself – and the way in which he said 'Mummy' had that ring to it just now.

I made eye contact with him in the rear-view mirror as I drove. 'Yes, Tobes?' I asked.

'Mummy, if I wasn't alive, you'd be so much happier.'

I frowned. *Where was this going? Toby* was *alive so there was no* … But his next words cut my thought process stone-cold dead.

'Perhaps if I jumped off a cliff …' he said.

A stillness settled on the car. The other kids went quiet; I think I forgot to breathe.

'Toby,' I said slowly, deliberately. I tried to frame it in language he would understand. 'Tobes, if you died, I'd be broken-hearted *for the rest of my life*.'

'Oh,' was all he said. 'Oh, I am sorry.'

He turned and looked out the window, his features unreadable. Outside, the Oxfordshire countryside flashed past the windows: so very ordinary. I realised my heart was pounding. My little boy was four years old, and he was talking about killing himself. It was so awful my brain almost couldn't compute what had just happened.

I didn't say anything to my mum when I got there. I didn't want to upset her. Instead, I tucked the memory away inside me, where it sat alongside memories of my dad.

Every single one of them cut me like a knife.

8

New Discoveries

'Wakey, wakey, kids, rise and shine!'

September 2009. It was Toby's first day at school; in the same building as the pre-school he'd attended, but this year he would be in the reception class. That morning, I hoped he *would* literally take me at my word as I called for the kids to get up for school; I hoped he would rise above all his struggles this coming year, and shine like the star I knew he was.

We'd had a very good summer. We always take a holiday in France – it's what Neil lives for throughout the year – and we'd bought a family caravan just before Ollie was born that got a lot of use. All the kids had enjoyed their breaks from school or nursery, though, for Toby, I'm afraid I had insisted on *some* lessons. Every holiday now, I'd decided, I was going to choose a problem he had, some area of life that he found difficult, and work on it with him throughout the vacation. That summer holiday, we'd talked about idioms, and how people don't always say as they mean. Toby had had an incident with one of the dinner ladies, you see, when she'd been counting up the children and had told him, 'You're a hot dinner.'

'I'm not a hot dinner,' Toby had responded.

'You *are* a hot dinner,' she'd insisted, checking her notes.

They'd gone back and forth like this for a while. I can still remember him coming home, all confused, and saying, 'But Mummy, I'm *not* a hot dinner. I'm Toby!'

So we'd worked on idioms, and I had all sorts of ideas for what we could do next. Jokes, I thought, would be a good one. That would hopefully help him to fit in a little better, maybe even make some friends.

He was still a very insular boy. At Lauren's birthday party in August, which we'd held in a big school hall, he'd sat the whole time in this little side room, which we'd used to prepare all the party food. Games were going on in the main hall, but Toby chose to sit in the side room out of the way and play with one of our phones, rather than join in. I hoped maybe that would change this year, as he became a little more mature and we helped him with his understanding of relationships, but only time would tell.

Neil and I had tried to prepare him as much as possible for 'big school'. We'd taken photographs of his new classroom and his teachers – he would be leaving Hannah (and me) behind in the pre-school and have a new class teacher this year – and we had explained very clearly what would be happening, and why, and when. So it wasn't quite an alien world that I took him into, as I ushered him into a classroom with a pink carpet and a blue rug, with blinds on the windows and blue plastic chairs. But he still seemed very uncertain about it all.

The slow process of securing a formal diagnosis of autism was still continuing behind the scenes, but in the meantime he had a new IEP (Individual Education Plan) for this term, and to begin with he started very well, getting smiley faces from his teacher for trying to respond in a positive way to her commands. But then it all got a bit too much again. He started shouting out at carpet time; he refused to get changed for PE. Change in general was a big problem for him, whether the children were changing clothes or rooms or simply changing their environment from the playground to the classroom. I guess he anticipated what was coming: the noisy classroom, and the cloakroom where he'd have to hang up his red coat with its snug little hood that kept him feeling safe, and how the cloakroom would be busy and full of children shoving and pushing their way along. Change and noise always seemed to set him off, like a twisted short fuse on a bomb. And when the gunpowder went *boom*, this red mist would come over him and he seemed to lose all power of thought and speech.

I'd talk to Toby after these meltdowns – a kind of debrief, as after a terrorist attack – and he would be unable to remember what had happened. Normally, he was a very articulate boy and could tell me how he was feeling and why and what had 'provoked' his explosion of anger, but sometimes with these red-mist episodes he couldn't even remember the chain of events. All sense would leave him. It was as though he was a miniature Incredible Hulk (but much less green), where Toby would assume these violent and destructive superpowers, yet have no idea of what he had done when he later 'came to'. Because he was so articulate normally, often his teachers expected him to be able to explain, even in the moment of his rage, but it was like all his words just went when the red mist came; they evaporated into nothingness within the scarlet fog. The school never seemed to grasp the sensory overload that had prompted the meltdown in the first place and so often they tried to talk to him and hold him still. They were only doing it out of the goodness of their hearts but, actually, another voice in his ear was the last thing Toby needed, and their intervention frequently made it worse. Though we explained the best way to deal with him, in the heat of the moment our advice was sometimes lost as the normal approach would be to talk a child down and the staff understandably acted instinctively.

I should add I never saw these meltdowns myself; not when Toby was that age, at least. They never happened at home, where he still remained mostly calm and docile, and we were able to ensure his strops didn't escalate; they only ever happened at school.

One day, during that first term of his reception year, I got a call to come in and help Toby. He'd had another meltdown, and this one had been *really* big – so big that the teacher had had to clear *all* the children out of the classroom and move them into another one, because it wasn't safe to leave a single child in the same room as my son. (You can imagine how that must have made him feel.) He had kicked and screamed and thrown things; he had raged and wailed at the top of his voice. It was like an extreme temper tantrum, which I guess is similar to an extreme storm: violent, unexpected, occasionally catastrophic – but, eventually, it will blow itself out.

When I got there, Toby was sitting in the corner of the classroom. He was hunched over and his face was turned away from me. He was almost growling. When he turned to face me, his lips were curled back and he snarled. Although taken aback at the venom in his expression, I didn't let it show. Instead, I sat down on a chair close to him and I said, 'Hello, Tobes, are you all right, lovely?' I didn't say anything more.

You could see him slowly, physically calm down. It took some time, but after a while the snarl faded from his lips and his shoulders softened and relaxed. I'd always said to him – to *all* my children – 'I'm your Mummy, I'm your advocate. Do you know what "advocate" means? It means I'm always here and, if you can't say it, I'll say it for you. I will always make sure that you are heard. And if you've done wrong, we'll sort it out. And if you feel you've been done wrong by, we will sort it out. I'm here to be your advocate, that's my job.' I think Toby remembered those words and had that trust; he knew I was there to try to make it better.

As he wound down, I could see him start to change. The Incredible Hulk vanished, and there was Toby again, intelligent and curious and very sweet-natured. We spent some time talking with his teacher, and Toby was like a different child now he'd calmed down. With my prompting, he said 'sorry' to the teacher and then he came home.

It would have been all right if we could have learned from each episode, but other than serving to catalogue yet another trigger, we learned nothing: the meltdowns just kept coming and there seemed no way of stopping them. And there were other incidents, too. I got a call one day to say Toby had hit and bitten two older boys in the playground. Off the record, the teacher told me they had chased him and were trying to get something off him, and they'd pinned him down and trapped him until he fought back as only Toby knew how. I don't want to sound like a parent who thinks their child's an angel because I know he's not, but on this occasion it did sound like he'd been backed into a corner until he felt there was no other way out. It's very hard as a parent to hear that, particularly as Toby, of course, was told off and subsequently disciplined for his violent behaviour.

In fact, Toby always seemed to be being told off. Given he had no inkling of changes in tone, I suppose it wasn't surprising that his default position became to assume that *anything* anyone said to him was intended as a criticism. Just as a reminder, I might say to all the kids, 'Don't forget to clear your plates from the table,' and immediately he'd start defending himself. I might say, 'Come on, Tobes, put your shoes on,' and he'd give me an angry response.

'Why are you shouting at me?' I'd ask.

'Because you're cross with me,' he'd reply, when nothing had been further from my mind.

Life must have been so confusing for him. People were so unpredictable; he had no idea what was coming next. We took to telling him 'I'm not cross' or, conversely, 'I'm serious now,' because otherwise Toby had no clue. We literally had to tell him how we were feeling because no facial expression or gesture or tone would convey it to him otherwise.

At school, however, more often than not people *were* cross with Toby. And everyone knows that children learn by copying others. After a while, I suppose it was inevitable that he would start to become cross with himself.

It was a cold December day, just before Christmas, when he came home with an injury. I knew he'd had a tricky day – he hadn't shared a toy or something like that; it wasn't a particularly huge disaster – but there hadn't been a report of any fights, so I was surprised to see a big bite mark on his arm when he rolled up his sleeve. It was swollen and red. This was a day not long after the trouble with the older boys in the playground, so my hackles immediately rose in Toby's defence, but I didn't want to say, '*Who* did that?' because that sounded so accusing. Instead, I said lightly, as though it wasn't a big deal, as though it wasn't obvious someone had clamped their teeth on his fragile limb, 'What's happened there?'

Toby glanced down at his pale arm, where a circle of teeth marks rose clearly from the surface of his skin: a stone circle of pain and hurt. He looked back up at me solemnly. 'I was really cross with myself, Mummy,' he simply said.

Oh, Tobes. I let out an unwilling sigh, a puff of breath to try to steady my nerves. I couldn't bear the idea of him hurting himself.

I sat down slowly at the table beside him, trying to gather my thoughts. *How can I respond to this?*

'Toby, we don't hurt ourselves when we're cross,' I explained carefully, making sure to enunciate each word. *Please let him understand.* 'Think of another way. If you're feeling cross with yourself, what's the best thing you can do? Perhaps if you went into the quiet corner and read a book, or had a run round outside or something like that. We don't hurt ourselves. OK?'

His eyes were on mine, his expression serious. 'But I felt I needed punishing.'

He was so matter-of-fact about it; it was just awful.

Not knowing what else to do, I got out the first-aid kit and rubbed some arnica into the wound. I only wished that I could make his brain better with a simple dab of cream; not to change who he was, you understand, because I loved Toby for being Toby, but just to make sure he *understood* that he shouldn't hurt himself any more. If only it was that easy …

After that incident, I was always looking out for injuries. And there they were, again and again. No matter what Neil or I said to Toby, he would still hurt himself when he was cross; when he felt he'd done something wrong. He might come home with a bump on his head where he'd walloped himself with something hard, or a scratch or a bite or a bruise. Sometimes the injury would happen during a meltdown, but at other times he'd actually take himself away from the classroom to hurt himself – so on some occasions the school wouldn't even have been aware of the injury until we asked them what the trigger had been this time …

Over the Christmas holidays, I noticed Toby started hitting himself if I told him off. I might be saying, 'Toby, don't do that!' and then he'd slap himself, *hard*, in the face. His palm would make a ringing sound as it connected with his cheek, and his skin would bloom red under his fingers. It was a really hard thing to witness. As Neil and I were both adamant that Toby had to be accountable for his behaviour, we couldn't stop telling him off to avoid such scenes. After all, even if you have a 'problem', a condition, you still need to know when a certain action is the wrong thing to do. Having grown up with a brother with special needs, I was very aware that it was important to treat all our children the same – not only because it wasn't fair on Toby's siblings if he was allowed to get away with things they weren't, but also because we were raising him to become an adult. And if unaccountable children grow up to become unaccountable adults, it is not a good outcome. Hard as it was, we had to tell Toby off if he was doing something he shouldn't – but it was *horrible* because he would literally hit himself right in front of us as a result. It became almost a natural movement for him as soon as the words 'No' or 'That's not quite right' were said to him. He would also be quick to react if ever he thought he had hurt someone else.

That Christmas of 2009, Toby, once again, was sick. By now, we had become aware that this was a pattern, together with illness on his birthday. And as we had grown to understand Toby better over the past year, it was a pattern we now recognised and understood. For Toby, change is his Kryptonite. So any days that are *different* are days that make him anxious and on edge. On his birthday, when everybody would say to him, 'Oh my goodness, it's your birthday, it's so special, you're going to have such a great day …' the pressure of expectation and the *difference* produced by the associated presents and cakes and balloons made it a great big stress-ball day for him. And at Christmas, when not only his family but the entire Western world went excitement-mad, counting down the days to 25 December with increasingly fevered anticipation, his panic was even worse. He would get snappy and edgy the closer the date got, and eventually he would be physically ill – my poor boy.

This was the year we decided things would have to be different; we couldn't put him through it again. After all, the expectation everyone pins on certain days to be different is simply engineered; no day is *really* any different to any other. From that year onwards, we decided Toby's anxiety was too much; that the festivities weren't worth it. We did still put up a tree and I still did Advent for the children and things, but we made sure not to make it a big excited drama any more. We tried to make it as chilled and calm as we could, and much more toned down. And we hoped for the best.

I think the other children understood; I *hope* they did. Quite early on we explained to Lauren and Joe that Toby needed a bit of extra help at school and that some of the things we were doing were to try to make him happier; it was always clear to them (and probably the entire neighbourhood …) when Toby wasn't happy, and how serious that could be. We didn't go into huge detail, but we knew the kids, especially Lauren, could be worriers, and we wanted them to understand as much as they could.

Though we got them involved with some of our tasks – for example, thinking of things we could add to Toby's 'I can' book – we were also careful that they never felt accountable for him or his behaviour. I'd never ask Lauren to keep an eye on her brothers, because I never wanted her to feel she had to look after anyone but herself. When you're a child, you shouldn't have to be responsible for another child – at least that's what I felt. That said, after Lauren found out about Toby, she always wanted to help in any way she could; she is that kind of girl.

Nonetheless, despite both of them being understanding and helpful, it *was* difficult for them, as well as Ollie. Toby would be praised and rewarded for doing little things that were second nature to the others – such as sharing, or being nice to relatives – but their best behaviour was taken as read and even expected. I think as they grew older they understood more, but it was harder for the younger boys. With all the upheaval of the past year, Joe had become a lot quieter, I'd noticed. It was difficult to say why. It could have been that Toby's dramas meant Gobby the Hobbit couldn't compete; or it could have been that school itself had curbed his excess chatter, because at the start of his school career he'd spent an awful lot of time by the yellow door for talking too much, but that didn't happen anymore. Instead, following in his sister's footsteps, he became a quiet, academic child, focusing on his passions, which were science and tech. Joe was a plodder, and he always just put his head down and got on with his life.

The school year drew on, for Joe and Lauren and Toby alike. And then, in April, we had a breakthrough. I was absolutely stunned when Toby – for the first time ever – mentioned another child by name. It was a *huge* step forward for us.

Up until then, Toby had only seemed to interact with other people in a slightly inappropriate manner; for example, he would mirror what I did but it would come out wrong – so I might hug a friend whose daughter was having a baby, rubbing her arm affectionately and saying, 'Oh, that's really lovely,' but then Toby would do *exactly* the same thing, as though he was a thirty-something mother-of-four who'd been her friend for decades. It was odd. Alternatively, he was fond of kissing and tickling his classmates, just as he did with his brothers and sister, not realising that this wasn't the way most people behaved with non-family members on an everyday basis. It was sweet, especially in a five-year-old, but it wasn't quite *right*.

Yet one April playtime I saw from my pre-school classroom – which was next to the main school playground – that Toby wasn't lining up (as usual) but was swinging on some metal bars. Always trying my hardest to help him manage his way in the world, I stuck my head out of the door and whispered to him, 'Tobes, go and line up.'

He assessed the line of children. 'Can I stand near Peter?' he asked.

I almost did a double-take; I was so surprised he was even aware of somebody else's name!

'Of course you can!' I said brightly.

'Peter's really sad,' he commented to me – and, indeed, there was a small blond boy crying in the line. 'He's missing his mummy,' Toby went on, 'Peter is really, really sad because his mummy's gone away on business and he's missing her, so I'm having to look after him.'

Well, I never …

With that, he ran off and lined up next to Peter. I thought that was so nice of Tobes to have that understanding of that little boy.

In fact, it was a level of emotional empathy of which I had never before known he was capable.

I watched Peter closely, mindful of some of the other kids' reactions in the past to my 'red-mist' son, but he smiled at Toby as my boy ran up to him, and made space for him in the line. Later, I would meet him myself, and find him to be a really gentle, lovely child, very accepting of others.

After that, it was 'Peter this' and 'Peter that' and 'Peter's my best friend' from Toby. It was almost too much; he seemed a little obsessed, almost as if he was relying on Peter for all friend-related activities and comments. And while Peter was always friendly to him, I was almost certain his mum didn't hear 'Toby this' and 'Toby that' from noon to night.

But you know what? I didn't care a jot. My son Toby had a friend, Peter. I felt like the proudest mother on the planet. And, with the wind in my sails, I made more positive discoveries, such as the power of audiobooks. We used to listen to these in the car: the Roald Dahl books on CD. To be honest, we'd be listening and find the trip we were taking wasn't long enough for an entire chapter, or a complete book, and so we used to sit on the drive, the four kids and me, for a whole hour after we got home, waiting for the end of the story because we wanted to find out what had happened! Anyway, we all loved the books, but Toby's engagement with them was something else. He'd listen to them so intently that he'd zone out completely. If you talked to him while they were playing, he didn't hear you because his ears would be channelled into the narrator's voice to the exclusion of all else. This, in a child who found the smallest noise to be a horrible distraction! It was like the audiobooks created a bubble in his head in which only he and the story existed, and his other sensory issues didn't disturb him there, as long as he was listening. They were a complete godsend.

I was feeling reasonably confident that we were managing Toby as well as could be expected. Look at him: he was making friends; we were adapting our lives to help him, such as understanding the pressures of 'special' days; and we were discovering more and more tricks to help him through the world. He did still have meltdowns at school, and he still said he felt ill before going in each day – from the anxiety of what might go wrong for him and what he might be expected to do – but I hoped with time that would improve. At least he was reasonably well behaved at home.

It was with all this in mind that Neil and I felt confident enough to leave him and his siblings with their grandma one afternoon while we just popped out. We didn't really leave the kids that often, to be honest, but we did this one time, and it felt lovely to step out just the two of us, like old times. I linked my arm in my handsome husband's and we waved goodbye to the kids quite happily, confident all would be OK.

I think we were only out for about an hour, if that. When we returned, the front door was locked.

'That's odd,' I said to Neil. I fished my keys from my bag and opened up.

There was a weird atmosphere in the house; I could tell right away. Lauren and my mum must have heard my key in the lock because they rushed into the hallway and Lauren ran straight into my arms for a hug. She was very upset. My mum looked ashen-faced and they were both clearly shaken.

'What's all this, then?' said Neil. 'Everything OK?' Perhaps unwittingly, he cast his eyes upwards, to where Toby's bedroom door was shut tight against the world.

My mum and Lauren told us what had happened. How they'd been trying to organise a family game for them all, and Toby had got stressed out about it. He liked his structure, you see, and his rules; he was the type of boy who, if he saw someone pushing into a queue, he would march straight up to them and call them on it. Rules were rules were rules. So family games did sometimes cause problems, because if anyone wanted to be imaginative with how the game was played, or if the rules were ever bent or exceptions made, Toby would kick off as the family's self-appointed dictator-referee.

But, on this occasion, he had completely lost it. He had hurled all the toys in the playroom all over the floor – heavy toys: thick plastic trucks and hardback books and massive fire engines. Things that had sharp edges and dead weights. Everything was dragged off the shelves and flung mindlessly around the room. Grandma had been shouting to Lauren, 'What do I do? What do I do?' but neither one of them could do anything to calm him down. When they tried to restrain him, he kicked and wriggled and writhed until they'd had to back off. In the end, they'd had to leave him to it, to the crashing and banging and hurling, even though both of them were worried he would hurt himself with all the heavy things he was flinging around.

And then, as they discussed whether to ring us or what to do next, Toby came tearing out of the playroom and tried to get out of the front door. Grandma saw him putting his shoes on, ready to storm out, and with quick thinking locked the door. Toby yanked the handle over and over, and then stormed round the house searching for the keys, throwing more things to the ground as he did so. He'd been yelling his head off and shouting at Grandma and Lauren and Joe and Ollie, using aggressive, hateful words that stung. And all the while he was snarling and shouting, curling up his top lip, baring his teeth. Eventually, he'd retired to his bedroom and slammed the door, and that was where he was now, simmering away behind the closed door.

I could tell they were completely shell-shocked. I hugged Lauren back and told them both they'd done the best they could and they could have done nothing more. Then I thanked Mum for looking after the children and I made sure Ollie and Joe were OK. While Neil made Mum a cup of tea and tried to carry on with 'normal' life for the others, I checked on Toby – a new bite mark bloomed on his bruised forearm, freshly made – and tried to reassure him that he wasn't bad; he'd just made some bad choices. We talked through how the day could have gone better, and what he could have done instead, and how he might choose to behave in the future. I settled everyone down, and a kind of unhappy calm returned to the house.

And I knew we'd made another discovery about Toby that day.

Neil and I could never, ever leave him on his own again. One of us would *always* have to be with him.

9

Diagnosis

We stuck to our word. In short, we didn't think the responsibility of looking after Toby should lie with anyone else. We always felt that we had been dealt this situation, so *we* should deal with it. Once we knew he couldn't be left with anyone else and needed to be with us, we never questioned that it was ever going to be any other way. This was what we'd been served, and it was just the way it had to be.

That's not to say it was easy. It was a time in our lives when friends and family were getting married, and invitations to once-in-a-lifetime weddings would drop through our letterbox. Whenever we received an invite to anything – whether it was a wedding or a large family picnic or a reunion with friends – the discussion between Neil and me was: 'Who's going?' It wasn't: 'We're all going'; it was: 'Who's going?' We did everything on our own. One of my best friends got married that same summer, and I remember attending on my own. It was hard, because those are the kinds of things you want to do together, as husband and wife. I remember sitting at the wedding, surrounded on all sides by couples, and surreptitiously extracting my phone from my handbag.

Wish you were here, I texted Neil. *It would be so lovely if you were here.*

I wish I was too, he replied, a moment later. And then: *I miss you.*

I miss you too …

After the summer, it was back-to-school time again. Toby was in Year One; Lauren in Year Nine; Ollie, then aged two and a half, was at a nursery while I continued my part-time job at the pre-school; and Joe was entering Year Seven, his first year at the same secondary school as Lauren. Toby was immediately put on his latest IEP. These were ongoing reports, every term, and generally for each report he would have a new area to work on. For example, the teachers, with our support, were trying to teach him that kissing and tickling his classmates was inappropriate, and that he must ask the children if they wanted to be tickled before he stretched out his fingers and wiggled them into their sides. He had learning points about getting changed before and after PE in a timely and sensible manner; about not shouting out; about following an adult's instruction *even when he didn't agree with it*; about using coping strategies to try to calm himself down before a meltdown occurred (deep breathing exercises and going to a quiet place with his things). By now he had learned not to bite other children – to my enormous relief – but he still threw things when he got cross, including chairs and even tables, which of course had the *potential* to hurt others if they were accidentally in the firing line. Although to my knowledge no one had ever been hurt by Toby in this way, both the school and I were concerned that it might be an accident waiting to happen.

It was an awful lot of stuff for a confused little boy to get his head around, not to mention his trying to take in all the usual mind-blowing education a child has to cope with, especially as they move from the more relaxed reception class to the formal education of Year One. For alongside learning all of the above, which were social skills Toby really struggled with, he also had to focus on forming his letters, picking up maths, developing his language and spelling, and comprehending the broad array of primary-school education: science, art, geography, history, IT and more … To my immense pride, he did really, really well at the educational side of things. English was always a bit tricky because of the whole 'understanding the concept' of it, and he found handwriting difficult as his motor skills were a little behind, but in all the rest he was pretty much ahead of his classmates and his understanding, especially of science and maths, was huge.

One thing kept coming up again and again on the IEPs, though: 'I will improve my self-confidence'. This was one area in which Toby never seemed to make progress.

I wish I could have helped him more; I saw first-hand how his struggles at school impacted on him. Every evening was a process of repair. I would spend hours with him after school, sitting up in his room and trying to reassure him. He would say that he didn't deserve to be loved and that he didn't deserve my help because he was a bad person. He would bite and hit himself. He would say I would be better off and happier if he was dead. It was just so sad. Each afternoon, I felt I was simply sticking him back together so that he could face another day. Sometimes I found myself holding him on my knee, quietly crying above his huddled little body – so quietly he wouldn't be able to tell – just hoping that I could physically hold all the broken pieces together and somehow make everything OK.

And then another day would dawn and Toby would start it by feeling ill. He would have to sit with a bowl while the household around him was getting ready for school, or he'd sit on the loo with an upset tummy. There was never anything medically wrong with him; it was all down to his anxiety. I hated having to take him in, but I just thought, *We need to do this. Hopefully if we go and have a success today, then it will be all right.*

Some days were a success. On others, I would receive a phone call to come and help; calls that got more and more regular as time went by. If I wasn't working, I would rush straight from our home to the school, taking Ollie with me; I would bring a snack and a toy for my youngest boy and try to treat it as an 'outing'. If I was at work, I would have to make my apologies, leave the class I was assisting and get to Toby's classroom as quickly as I could. I was lucky that I worked in the same school that Toby attended, so my unscheduled departures were not a huge issue; my colleagues were incredibly understanding about it all.

It always happened the same way: as soon as I walked in, I could visibly see his relief that someone who understood him had arrived. It would take a couple of minutes for him to chill out because he was so uptight and feeling so upset, but then his body would relax and he would come and give me a cuddle and then we would be able to go and say our sorries to everybody.

I had to teach him to say sorry. Like idioms and jokes, he didn't understand what it meant. We taught him that saying sorry repairs people's feelings. So if you've done something that might have hurt their feelings, if you say sorry that makes it better. I could tell he was doing it only because I'd asked him to, but I hoped that, if I kept on with him, full understanding would follow.

Year One was proving very, very hard for him. It didn't help that Toby had two class teachers that year, who were job-sharing. That was extremely difficult because they were both very different teachers. If change was Toby's Kryptonite, then in Year One he lived on a planet where the very soil was made of it. School life didn't have the consistency he needed; the rules, to him, seemed to change from day to day.

I know the school tried their very best. Pam in particular was excellent. It was just that they had never had a child such as Toby attend before; not one who had these special needs. The staff were just being teachers and trying to do what they could to help him learn – but they would force him to do things as a normal child would have to, and it was simply beyond him. It would be things like … he didn't want to stay in the classroom because it was too noisy and busy. And they'd say – as though this was a solution – 'You can sit on a chair in the classroom' (as opposed to on the carpet). But the issue was the classroom itself, so while it was really nice that they were offering him a chair, it wasn't what he needed and so he couldn't cope and then he would melt down, or kick out – or run off. For Toby had started bolting at school now, too, and that was another increasing concern.

The term drew on, and things with Toby grew worse and worse. When he had his sixth birthday, on 14 October 2010, for the first time we didn't even tell him that 'today is the day'. I was so sad about that, because as a mother I wanted to make that day special for him and to have that build-up and excitement, to make lovely childhood memories for him, but we just couldn't. We offered him a party, and to begin with he was quite up for it; but the closer his birthday got, the more stressed out he became, and in the end he just said, 'No thanks, Mummy.' I think he wanted to, but I don't think he felt able to cope with it. So Toby turning six came and went, and for the first time in years he wasn't poorly on the day, because he didn't know on the day that it was supposed to be special.

On 9 December 2010, we finally had our first formal meeting at an NHS hospital about Toby's 'potential' autism, which was arranged for us via our GP. It couldn't have come soon enough. That whole term, I felt as though my son was being destroyed. It was like he was a square peg and the school were knocking him into a round hole – and every single time they tried to hammer him into place, they knocked bits off him. Though I tried my best to stick him back together each evening, I could see how he was splintering and falling apart, and it just broke my heart. I only hoped that getting a formal diagnosis would help to secure for him the specialist support he so desperately needed.

The woman we saw at the meeting, a psychiatric nurse called Kat, could not have been lovelier. She was really bubbly, and so good at talking to Toby. She asked him questions in a very open way, and even though we could tell she was testing him at the same time, she had such a good manner that Toby chatted away quite happily to her. I remember she wanted him to draw a picture, and he insisted on using a yellow pen and wouldn't change his choice, even when she asked him to use another because, she explained, she would have to photocopy his picture and the yellow pen wouldn't show up. Toby, as he always did in such situations, dug his heels in and said, 'No!' But instead of squishing him and forcing him to do as she asked, she simply said, 'Let's go and test it, shall we?' And when Toby saw for himself that the yellow didn't work, he agreed to switch to a blue pen. She did those sorts of go-the-extra-mile things; she was really nice.

I remember her asking Toby, 'What are your problems?'

He gave a big sigh of self-loathing. 'I would get tired if I listed them *all*,' he said.

That made my heart ache – he just didn't believe in himself. But in the next breath he made me smile.

'What would you like to be when you grow up, Toby?'

'I'm considering some future jobs,' he said thoughtfully. 'Secret agent, scientist, army person, footballer …'

That last was a strange one, because he didn't join in with the football at school. He and Peter played together occasionally, but they'd play things like being Transformers. Toby found some physical tasks difficult and so he tended to avoid sporting activities, such as riding a bike or playing footie. Peter, in contrast, was a sporty boy. He still seemed Toby's only real friend, at least to me, but when Kat asked about his friendships, Toby stated that all the people at school were his pals.

'How do you know that, Toby?' Kat asked.

'I love them,' he replied. He had such a big heart. That was a very telling answer, though – it was all about how *he* felt about them, rather than how *they* might feel about him.

He still found it very difficult to understand other people and their feelings, despite his flash of insight about Peter being upset.

That term, one of his teachers had told me that Toby had been present when a little girl had had an accident; she had fallen off a chair and hurt herself quite badly. Immediately, she had started crying and screaming. The other children present had expressed concern for her well-being, but Toby had reacted by clamping his hands over his ears and complaining about the noise.

We told Kat about that, afterwards; we'd made a whole list of observations about Toby for our GP, which was passed on to her too.

After the meeting, she said she had seen all she needed to in order to take us forward to the next stage of the process, and she referred us to a consultant for further investigation. Neil and I put the date of the next meeting in our diaries and hoped for the best: 10 February 2011 could be a date that changed everything.

And it was.

I remember being scared before we went in. I was so worried the doctor would just say, 'There's nothing wrong with him.' We'd had to jump through so many hoops and see so many specialists and fill in so many forms even to get to this point, and I was really anxious that we might go through all that and then not get the answer we needed. Up to that point, we were never given anything for free, everything was a battle, and I just hoped against hope that the diagnosis would be forthcoming and we would get Toby the help he needed.

The consultant we saw had a reputation for being tough. I was warned about her beforehand, which didn't help my nerves. I had mentioned to someone which doctor we were seeing, and they'd said, 'Oh, getting a diagnosis out of her is very hard.' So

I was extremely nervous the day we took Toby to meet her. This was it.

The consultant was a very professional lady with dark curly hair and olive-toned skin. She asked questions all the time, and made notes we couldn't read. And while a letter would later come in the post to back up her informal conversation, she did give Neil and me her diagnosis there and then.

'My impression of your son,' she said to us, 'is that Toby is presenting with social communication difficulties. All of this points in the direction of Autistic Spectrum Disorder, Asperger's syndrome.'

Woah. I felt really emotional hearing her say the words. Even though I knew in my heart there was a problem, hearing someone so qualified tell me that what I'd suspected was absolutely true was very overwhelming.

'Toby is functioning well in terms of his academic abilities,' she went on. I nodded; yes, he was a bright little thing, he really was. 'But,' she added, and here her expression finally softened, 'he is significantly socially impaired.'

She wrote down the title of a book for us to read; I think it was one I already had in my huge stack. 'Read this,' she said, 'it's very interesting.

'He will probably become depressed when he's a teenager, so come back then.'

And that was that. Kat and the consultant worked for the Child and Adolescent Mental Health Service (CAMHS), and with Toby not being clinically depressed, they now discharged him from their care. We would have support from the Autism Advisory Service, but that was it. Finally getting the diagnosis was great after so long – because we could now say, officially, 'Yes, there is something wrong with our child and we can now sort it out' – but it also felt rather like they'd washed their hands of us. 'There's your diagnosis, off you go!'

Neil and I discussed at length whether or not to tell Toby. At first, we didn't; we just waited. This was partly because our own emotions were all over the place and we needed to get them in check before we could talk to him rationally, as we needed to, but we were also worried about telling our insecure little boy that there was something 'wrong' with him. In the end, though, we did sit him down to have a conversation about his diagnosis.

'Toby, do you remember going to see the doctor at the hospital?' I asked, as he sat on the sofa beside me, flapping a little and wriggling his hands.

'Yes, Mummy,' he said. Toby had an excellent memory.

'Well, she has told us what she found out about you from her tests,' I continued brightly. 'What she found out is that your brain works in a different way to other people's.'

Toby didn't react.

'Sometimes,' I said carefully, 'this means there will be things that you don't understand as well as other people do. But it also means there will be some things you can do *better* than others.'

Toby still didn't say anything.

'This won't stop you doing *anything*, Toby,' Neil added. 'This doesn't change who you are.'

'You're still great and you're still amazing …' I chipped in.

'… And we will try to do everything in our power to help you when you need help,' Neil finished.

We looked at our son but he didn't say very much at all. He waited till we'd finished and then he looked up and opened his mouth to speak.

'Oh, OK,' he said. 'Can I go and play with my Lego now?'

And with that he disappeared up into his room and closed the door.

10

~

Something's Got to Give

It never rains but it pours. That same year, we found out that Joe was struggling with being bullied, just as Lauren had been before him.

He didn't say anything to us about it. Ever since Gobby the Hobbit had retired, Joe was an extremely quiet boy, almost monosyllabic. He rarely spoke up; he was the kind of child who, if he came to you and said, 'I feel a tiny bit under the weather,' it was grounds for rushing him straight to hospital, because he never, ever complained. He always said he didn't want any fuss.

We started to notice things weren't quite right. He seemed a very confident, self-assured boy on the surface but there were things that just didn't add up. He would come home with a huge grease mark on his shoulder, for example, and after a lot of wheedling and questions, he would finally admit someone had thrown a butter packet at him in the dinner hall. And it escalated from there, until people were shoving him in classrooms and he was coming home bruised. He even had his bag stolen by the bullies once; he came home empty-handed and even quieter than before. If ever I asked him, 'You all right, Joe?'

he'd simply reply, 'Yeah, I'm all right,' so I had to learn to ask the right questions. Once we'd wheedled out of him what was happening, he was a little more open, but he was never going to be a forthcoming child – one of those who comes and *asks* for your help. Instead, he internalised his problems and never liked to talk about anything personal. He always felt if he made a fuss then things might get worse.

Although we contacted the school and resolved the issues via the school welfare officer, once again I felt that I'd let my children down. It was such a horrible, horrible feeling. I was finding it harder and harder to juggle everything. Ollie was only three so he needed me in the way that little ones do; I'd been specially looking out for Lauren after her shaky start to secondary school; and Toby was so demanding with his after-school care and in-school emergencies I now realised Joe, bless him, had been left out a lot. He always insisted that he didn't need anything from me, and if ever I tried to help or discuss an issue, he'd just say, 'Go on, Mum. I'm fine. I don't want fuss.' It was hard to know if that was his true nature, or simply the way he'd turned out because of the family dynamics. What I did know was that he was now the quietest of all my children.

After the bullying was discovered, I told all the children we were going to start a new regime. Every child was going to have his or her own time slot, so they could have an opportunity to talk about their day (or, in Joe's case, I would get to *ask* him how he was, because he was never the chattiest). Ollie got time alone with me when I picked him up from nursery, and Toby would have the time straight after school. Lauren would see me as we were cooking supper or just before, and Joe would have the slot after dinner. Of course, if something urgent came up, the other children could come and ask for my help, but I only allowed interruptions if they were critical. Toby might rush into the kitchen when I was with Lauren because Ollie had messed up his line of cars or something, and I'd say, 'Is it *really* important what you need to say to me right now?' He'd shake his head. 'Then you need to let Lauren have her turn now, Tobes.' In time, he learned to grade his interruptions on a sliding scale: a ten would be 'we need to talk about it immediately'; a five, 'please can we talk about it this evening?' whereas below five was: 'in the next day or so, may we please discuss this?'

The new regime made things a little better, but as time went by and Toby continued to find school hard, there seemed to be fewer and fewer hours in the day. Every day, it seemed, there would be meetings about Toby at school. In the morning we'd be preparing for the day ahead and in the evening it would be a debrief; not to mention the times I got called in from work or home to smooth over some crisis or another. Sometimes I'd find myself talking to his SENCO Pam at 10 o'clock at night as we tried to solve Toby's problems. And even with our specified time slots for the children, if it had been a particularly bad day for Toby, I would have to spend longer than usual with Tobes in his room and so Lauren would tell Neil instead of me about her day. I felt bad about having to leave my work so often and bad about the other children missing out on their mother's time; I wasn't doing anything particularly well, I thought. I'm one of those '100 per cent' people; I wanted to give everything 100 per cent, but I was barely managing to scratch the surface. All I was doing was skimming the top, all the time, doing just enough to keep people going, but I wasn't solving anyone's issues. And as I moved from crisis to crisis and moment to moment, it felt like I was sticking a plaster on a problem but never having the time to work out what was really wrong.

It was an utterly overwhelming feeling. I sometimes felt that someone was physically draining everything out of me. Everything took so much *energy*. Having four children was always going to be busy, but it was the emotional cost that was the most tiring. Counselling Lauren and Joe when I could see they were both in pain. Worrying about Ollie growing up and my missing out on so much of his childhood, and what impact all this was having on him. And then there was Toby. I had to stay strong when he hit himself in front of me. I had to stay calm as he threatened to jump out of the window or throw himself off a cliff or in front of a car. I had to keep everything inside and never show how it all made me feel. I had to stay in control. I always thought, *If I'm not in control then my children are not going to feel very safe.* So it was always really important to me that they never, ever saw me cry.

But that didn't mean I didn't want to. Sometimes it was a daily battle to keep myself together. I was so busy that I found it was extremely rare for me to have any time on my own. There might be a five-minute gap between dropping Ollie off at nursery and my arriving at work, and I remember just crying all the way there because it was the only time I ever had through the whole week to just *feel* anything. I'd find myself on my own in the car and I would just cry. I'd get that physical *hurt* feeling inside, almost instantly, and the tears would come, and then as soon as I had to head into work it would be gone and I'd carry on.

I couldn't even rest at night. Toby had never been the best sleeper, frequently waking or getting up for a drink of water or a potter about in the loo or in his room, but as he became more and more anxious about school, he began to sleepwalk, too. I remember he scared the life out of Lauren the first time she saw it. She was coming up the stairs as Toby was coming down, and he stopped stock-still on the central step.

'Toby, are you OK?' she asked.

Slowly he turned his head towards her. Completely glassy-eyed, he was staring straight through her. He spoke softly: 'Yessssss.'

'*Mummy!*' she shouted, really creeped out. She thought he was really ill. 'Mum, come quick!'

I came running and saw Toby there with her, looking dazed. 'Toby, are you all right?'

'Yeah …'

'Toby, I think you're still asleep.'

No answer.

'Come on, shall we go back to bed?'

'Yeah …'

I took his arm, led him upstairs and put him back to bed, and then he settled down. But after that he would frequently sleepwalk and it was always at particularly stressful times at school.

We tried our hardest to make life as easy for him as possible. His sensory issues were a major problem for him, so we thought of ways to try to help him navigate the world that avoided meltdowns. Neil had a pair of yellow ear defenders that he used for his work at airports and he lent them to Toby. They cancelled out the noise around him and Toby loved them.

Inspired, we saved up and bought him a really expensive pair of good-quality headphones, a big black pair that went all the way over his ears and had a noise-cancelling button on them. Toby used to listen to his audiobooks through them too. We bought as many as we could as he just devoured them – the Harry Potter books, and the *How to Train Your Dragon* series. To begin with, he listened to them in his room to calm himself down, but we cottoned on that they provided a bubble he could take with him when he left the house. If he was protesting about making the journey to school, I'd say, 'Well, why don't you listen to your audiobooks?' And he'd go, 'OK.' And because the audiobooks meant he tuned out everything else around him, the journey would pass without incident.

He was in a complete bubble as we headed outdoors: the hood on his coat pulled up over his head, his sunglasses on, earphones plugged in. I used to have to steer him around, but sometimes it was the only way we could get him to go places.

Because it started to be not just school, but going *anywhere* that would give him the heebie-jeebies. And so that's how we went out, any time we left the house – because that was the *only* way we could get him out. He was totally zoned out to the world around him as he went. If he could have had eyes that turned inward so only the whites would show, that's what it was like: that total immersion in the world inside his head.

The only problem was, eventually I'd have to tell him we'd arrived at our destination, and he'd have to head into school. He began to be clingy, not wanting to leave me when we arrived at the school gates. He'd make a scene, and I'd smile self-consciously at the other parents standing alongside me at the gates. There was one really nice mum who still spoke to me, a woman called

Katie, and she would often come over and say hello. Toby would ignore her; he never said hello to anybody. But it was really nice for me to hear her loud, cheery voice calling hello. She's a very bubbly woman with kids of similar ages to mine, and her friendly face often gave me a boost, though I don't think she ever knew it.

The summer term arrived and Toby and I continued through the weekly onslaught of crisis and repair. I remember coming into school once that term after he'd had a meltdown and he was sat there in his jumper, with a bright-red face, his hair damp with sweat.

'Toby, you look really hot,' I said gently.

'I *am* really hot!' he shouted, his raised temperature making him extra grumpy.

'You've still got your jumper on,' I pointed out. 'Why don't you take it off?'

'Oh. OK.'

It really struck me that he hadn't connected the warm jumper with his hot feeling. For me this was another lesson in how to care for him. He had always been a hot bod, with sensitivity to heat even on moderate days, but I now realised I was going to have to help him with that. If I dressed him in a vest and T-shirt, I would write on his hand: *Remember you have a vest on.* Then he would know he could take his T-shirt off if he got too hot.

The older Toby got, the more I needed to do for him and the less independent he could be, it seemed. It was more pressure on me, but I braced my shoulders and tried to take the weight.

As the school year drew to a close, though, all of us panting over the finish line as though we were wearing thick woollen jumpers in the summer sun, I summoned up the courage to speak to Neil about it. As usual, I'd been keeping all the pressure to myself, but as I imagined myself starting yet another year of this horrendous juggling act, I knew something had to give. Any moment now, the balls were going to come tumbling down. It was time to sacrifice one of them.

'Neil,' I said one evening, as we tidied up the kitchen together at the end of the day. 'I just wanted to say ...' I took a deep breath; I didn't like talking about myself. 'I just wanted to mention that I'm finding it really difficult to balance it all, so I thought I might give up my job.'

'OK, fine,' he said. He was always supportive of anything I wanted.

'It's just, I've been reading, with kids with autism, if you can get as much work as possible done as early as possible with them, you make their life better when they're older. I feel if I can focus on Tobes as much as possible right now then we might be able to make things better in the future.'

'Yep, OK,' he agreed.

I felt relief – relief that I wouldn't be juggling another ball. I didn't think about the fact I was losing that precious time I spent on my own, or what else I might miss: the friendships of my colleagues and that community feeling I'd always enjoyed. I didn't even think about the fact my life would just be lived for the children now. If I had, I'd simply have thought, *That's what mothers do anyway*. I'd always put my needs on the back-burner, ever since Lauren was born, so I didn't even think about it: Toby needed me to do it, so I would do it. Everyone else came first.

I only hoped it would help.

11

~

Gone Too Far

Year One had been such a difficult year for Toby. Over the past 12 months, I had literally seen him diminish as a person to become this little stressball. I desperately wanted the summer to give him a reprieve, but unfortunately it didn't work out that way. When you have autism, there is no 'off' button. And Toby's condition seemed to be getting worse and worse.

We tried our hardest to give the kids a great holiday. I was still the same mum planning activities for them, though with Toby as he was I had to plan even more carefully. Did we have enough snacks, his audiobooks, his sunnies, water to cool him down? (Some summers he got so hot that I would literally have to pour water over his hair to give him some relief.) One sunny day that vacation, we braved the queues at Legoland.

We hadn't been there long when I saw Toby start to get agitated. He began by rocking back and forth on his heels as he stood in the queue for a ride.

'How long is it going to be, Mummy?' he whined.

'Quite a while yet, Tobes – see how long the queue is? But just think how fantastic the ride must be to have attracted so many children!'

He was quiet for about 30 seconds, and then he started up again. This time his body language grew tenser and he started wringing his hands and flapping. 'I'm hot, Mum. I'm thirsty. I'm hungry. I'm bored. How long is it going to be?' It was one thing after another: a litany of questions and complaints – constant, constant, constant. He didn't know what to do with his arms and legs, so he was wriggling, barely taking a breath between words.

I gave him a drink and he was quiet for about 20 seconds. Then: 'I can't wait any longer, Mum. We need to go now. I'm thirsty. I'm *so* thirsty. I'm so thirsty I could die! I'm going to die because I haven't got a drink!'

His voice was getting louder and louder. Even though I'd just given him a drink, he went on so much that in the end a lady at the side of him leaned over and offered him a beverage from her own cool bag. But it didn't calm him down; nothing did. And in the end he insisted: 'We need to go *now*. We'll go home *now*. We'll just go home.'

And so we did.

Another day, I took all the children to see the *Smurfs* movie. Toby wasn't a big fan of the cinema, because it was noisy and there were bright lights in his face, but I was conscious that it wasn't fair on his siblings not to go at all, so I tried really hard to make it a good trip for everyone.

It didn't go well – a bit hard-going is how I remember it. Ollie at three and a half was probably a little too young because he was bored, and I think Toby on this occasion was the most difficult he'd ever been in a cinema. We ended up being quite close to the screen because those were the only seats available, and it was bright and loud and it wasn't very good, and Toby got *really* wound up. In the end, I had to take Ollie and Tobes out into the lobby.

I leaned over to Lauren and Joe. 'You two stay and enjoy the film,' I whispered. 'I'll be just outside that door if you need me.'

I felt guilty for having to leave them, both because I always worry about their safety, even though Lauren was now fourteen, and because I wasn't experiencing the movie with them. I wanted to spend time with *all* my kids. It was so frustrating for me that we couldn't enjoy a simple day out together. For it was becoming a theme that, every time we went anywhere, I would end up having to calm Toby down on his own and the family would be split up. It was rare that we got to do anything together that lasted for the entire duration of the outing.

Being around other people reminded me how different our own situation was, too. That whole cinema was crammed with other families having a fabulous time, but for us it was a stressful event – and one that I knew would affect the rest of the day. For when we got home Toby would still be agitated and he'd be frustrated with himself for not coping with the cinema, and the rest of the day would be ruined.

I'd like to say that, as we headed off to France for our annual break, I hoped the change of scenery would do us all good, but of course change was always anathema to Toby. To help him, we went in the caravan, which was a 'home from home' for Tobes. He wouldn't have coped with the unfamiliar surroundings of a hotel or a *gîte*.

We went back to the same campsite too. It had a toddler pool the children liked that we'd realised in the past year or so we could clear within five minutes – thanks to Toby. He was such a stickler for rules that the moment he saw another child doing something wrong – splashing, or pushing in, or touching a button they weren't supposed to – he'd be straight up to their parent to point it out. 'Excuse me, do you realise that your child is doing such-and-such?' The parents, one by one, would take their children off until we had the place to ourselves.

Toby had no compunction about loudly pointing out other people's perceived faults too. In a supermarket, he might go up to a stranger with their basket of pizza and ice cream and say, 'Do you know your food is very unhealthy?' Or he might watch a passer-by waddle past and ask at the top of his voice, 'Mummy, why is that man so fat?' At first it was embarrassing, but he really couldn't help it. All I could do was try to help him learn – like I did with saying sorry, which we'd been working really hard on over the past year; and jokes; and sarcasm; and how to introduce yourself, which he now did with a handshake or a polite bow.

It was while we were in France that summer that I saw, for the very first time, one of Toby's red-mist meltdowns. Often he had 'moments' with us, don't get me wrong, but school had been telling me for years that these meltdowns were on a different level and now I saw exactly what they meant.

It happened at the campsite playground one afternoon. A group of kids, including my own, were all playing on this big slide: they'd go down the slide, run round to the ladder and climb up, and then go down the slide again. They'd been doing it for quite a while, over and over, and always in the same order. And then one child got in front of Toby and wrecked the beautiful symmetry of the afternoon.

I heard him yelling the moment it happened. And then he just … *ran*. I went after him and had trouble keeping up. You could see the stress and the power in him: there was so much that he looked as though he could take off. It was *absolute* – it took him over absolutely. I'd never seen anything like that in my life.

My reaction was simply to keep him safe. I'd learned not to talk to him when he was in a major strop because then you just added to the sensory overload he was experiencing, so I kind of left him for a bit, while keeping an eye on him. We were lucky, I think, that there was nothing nearby for him to throw. When he'd managed to calm himself down a little, I said to him, 'Tobes, let's go for a run.' And we ran round and round the football field together, trying to get rid of the rage and the pent-up angst that was still boiling away inside of him. He just kept saying over and over, like a mantra, 'He pushed in, he pushed in …' For him, the world was a strictly ordered place and this child had pushed it off its axis. He should therefore be punished. Toby couldn't understand why the entire global population wasn't up in arms about this terrible injustice.

Even once we got back home, Toby's bubbling anger didn't seem to subside. He would get angry at his siblings. He had learned it was wrong to physically hurt people, thank God, but he could still lash them with his tongue. And he said some pretty nasty things too. 'You're the worst sister in the world!' he might scream at Lauren. 'I *hate* you!' He picked up bad language – even though we tried to shield him from it, you can't stop up a child's ears in the playground – and so his rants would be peppered with F-words. He would yell with such venom, like he really meant it.

I know Lauren and the others were hurt by it, even though they knew Toby couldn't contain it. Afterwards, when he was calm, he would always apologise. You could tell he felt excruciatingly guilty and dreadful, and the siblings would hug each other with genuine contrition and forgiveness. But he couldn't take back the words he'd shouted with such aggression, as much as he now wanted to. Over time, I was aware of a kind of fracturing going on within the family that I absolutely hated.

Surely the new school year would be better than the last. *Surely*. I wouldn't have to worry about work, I could focus only on Toby, and I was certain that was going to make all the difference. I took the kids to buy their new school shoes before term began, and we all braced ourselves for the shopping trip as it was a sure-fire catalyst for a Toby wobble.

Knowing that, I tried to pick obscure times for the outing, like first thing on a Sunday morning or 6 p.m. on a Friday night, but back-to-school time is what it is, and whenever we went shoe shopping there always seemed to be a queue. And it was the waiting that was the problem. Sometimes, there would be an hour-and-a-half wait, with families crammed into the small shop and everyone noisy and stressed and irritable. It was manic.

Toby, knowing what was coming, was often stressed even before we left the house. He never saw the need to buy new shoes anyway, and would moan and whinge about it. Always he wanted the same shoes, so very often we would just buy the same design, simply in the next size up. I would park as close as I possibly could to the store and we'd walk along together as a family. The anxiety would make Toby very flippy-flappy, his nerves channelling from his brain along his limbs, resulting in a little kick out or an uncontrolled wave of his arm. I used to hold his hand and Joe would be nowhere near us – because he was embarrassed, I think. I had to hold Toby's hand in case he ran off.

That September, as usual, we entered the busy shoe shop and waited our turn. Chaos assaulted all our senses: the smell of new leather and stinky socks; the chatter of families and announcements from the staff; the sight of the new shoes and the flashing lights from the foot-measuring machine … Toby just didn't know what to do with himself, bless him. He tried to control his tension, but it was like this build-up and build-up of stress. You could see it taking him over: his shoulders got tense and his limbs shook and that top lip of his started to curl. He wriggled out of my hand and tried to leave the shop. Then he started crying.

'I don't want to do it, Mummy!' he wept. 'I want to go home!'

But his last pair of shoes was worn out and scuffed, and his feet had grown at least one size since the summer before.

'Sorry, Tobes, we've got to stay. But it won't be long now …'

'I don't *want* to!'

He was shouting at the top of his voice, tears streaking his angry red cheeks. All the other families turned and stared, and my lot all cringed inwardly. Buying shoes was the worst thing in the whole world for all of us, too. It was absolute hell.

And then the final torture for Toby: with all his senses assailed, he had to endure the touch of the new shoes as the assistant finally slid them onto his feet.

He grimaced, almost with pain. 'It doesn't feel right, Mummy,' he said. 'It's not comfortable.'

It was just because they were new – because they were *different*. We paid up and got out of there as quickly as we could. Of course, as soon as the shoes were worn in Toby was as happy as Larry about them. I only wished someone would invent a pair of shoes that grew with the child; it would have saved us an awful lot of upset.

New shoes always meant new term – and that September of 2011 I waved Toby off to his Year Two of school with hope in my heart. Little Ollie was at pre-school, Lauren in Year Ten and Joe in Year Eight. I hoped that we'd all soon settle into a nice, repetitive routine that would comfort Toby with its regularity.

I had good reason for my high hopes. Now Toby had his formal diagnosis, he had a teaching assistant (TA) assigned to him, who would be working one-on-one with him during the school day. Her name was Miss Ellis. I held my breath as I picked up Toby at the end of his first day and asked how it went. I knew he was meeting her for the very first time and I really hoped they had got on well. Toby could take against individuals from time to time, and he wasn't a boy who let his grudges go easily.

'So how was the teaching assistant, Tobes?' I asked.

'Miss Ellis?' he said. I nodded. 'Yeah, she's really nice.'

That was it – but that was a *fantastic* endorsement from Toby Turner. Personally, I was really impressed with her too. She was a lovely woman and very good with Toby. She used to wear her hair up in a ponytail, and trousers, trainers and a T-shirt top: the kind of outfit that said you were ready for anything, and she had to be with Toby.

Very quickly, though, things started to unravel. I think Toby was just so stressed about school that his tension was caused as much by the memories of everything that had gone wrong before as the new pressures being put upon him. Whatever the reason, it wasn't long before my phone started ringing with requests to come to the school. Miss Ellis was amazing, and Toby would sometimes run to her for help instead of running off, but not all the time – and those were the times when my phone would start to vibrate and the school's number would flash up on the caller ID and I'd know what was coming next.

To begin with, it was once a week, then twice a week … and before too long I was going in almost every day to sort out one problem or another. It got so bad that I found myself almost waiting for the phone to ring, whenever he was in school. If I was at home I'd have both my mobile and the house phone tucked in my pocket so I could answer the school's call for help as quickly as possible. Whenever I was out, I'd get in a panic if I went out of phone signal because I knew the school would need to ring. I never left Bicester, because it would have taken me too long to get back to Toby. Now I was on call 24/7 and I never knew quite what the next hour would bring.

Sometimes when I went in, I could calm him down and he would manage to carry on with his day. More often, I would have to take him home with me; giving up my job was proving to have been essential. The school, being understanding, arranged for Toby to start at different times to the other children, so that he didn't have to cope with the busy cloakrooms and all that noise and stress. I would take him in a little later, or lead him through reception rather than the playground, so the start to his day could be calm and quiet.

This meant, though, that I no longer saw Katie, or any of my other friends from the other kids' year groups, at the school gates. We were either getting in late or leaving early or having to attend meetings about Toby's behaviour at either end of the school day. That isolation was actually pretty hard. All the social side of school life was completely lost, full stop. I began to feel very, very alone. The only people I ever spoke to, adult-wise, were Neil and the staff at the school about Toby. There simply wasn't anybody else. In the end, my best friend ended up being the SENCO. And I'm not even joking.

Most mornings I used to cry in the shower, where nobody could see, the water streaming into my face and washing away the tears. I had to get it all out before I could paste on a bright smiley face for the children and Neil.

I never cried with Neil – or only rarely. He would get upset to see me upset, you see, so I felt I needed to be the strong one, to be the one who was organised. More than anything, I felt our fragile family would fall apart if *I* did, so I always kept everything bottled up and didn't let a single tear spill where anyone might see it.

As the term drew on and half-term hove into sight, Toby had yet another meltdown. I remember it specifically because of what happened at the school afterwards. I'd gone in to calm him down, and he had bravely pulled himself together.

'Shall we go and say sorry, Mummy?' he asked me, drying the tears on his cheeks.

'That's an excellent idea, Toby,' I replied. I was so proud of him for learning about 'sorry' – it had taken about eighteen months for us to get to this point.

He went up to the teacher to whom he needed to apologise. Of course his behaviour had been bad – I'm not making excuses for him. But he hadn't hurt anyone; he had just found it hard to cope and so he'd misbehaved and been disruptive.

He walked up to the teacher and tapped her on the arm in a very sensible fashion (no kissing or tickling). I could see the contrition in his eyes. I knew, later, that I would have to reassure him because he blamed himself for being a bad person and thought this was why things always went wrong for him. He cleared his throat.

'Miss,' he said. 'I just wanted to say I am very, very sorry.'

She turned and fixed her gaze on him. 'Toby Turner,' she said sternly. 'Saying "sorry" isn't good enough; you have to show me that you are sorry.'

It took my breath away. I just thought, *Do you know what? I've spent a year and a half trying to teach him to say sorry, and you've just destroyed that with your thoughtless words.* We didn't make a complaint; we did not have the energy for another fight.

Half-term couldn't come soon enough after that. We took the children to Longleat Safari Park in the caravan and camped in the grounds. As usual, it was very busy and Toby found it extremely difficult, but I remember that trip not for his meltdown, but for how he got himself out of one.

We'd just entered the 'hands-on' area, where you can stroke all the animals. Toby was very agitated and flappy and cross, but he kept himself together well enough to join a small group of children sitting on the floor with various creatures around them.

Toby's eye was caught by this huge monitor lizard. She was a beautiful creature with an angled head with sharp black eyes, sleek patterned skin, four legs and a long flicky tail. Toby reached out a tentative hand to her and gently ran his finger along her scaly skin. His shoulders seemed to sag a little from their previously uptight position. He stroked her again, more confidently this time. Again, his shoulders perceptibly lowered as I watched him from a corner of the room.

I think he must have sat there for fifteen or twenty minutes, just stroking that lizard constantly. It reminded me of when he listened to his audiobooks: you could see that everything around him disappeared and it was just Toby and the lizard, chilling out together. He had always been good with animals, but it was amazing to see how this animal was good for *him*. I found myself feeling strangely grateful to that scaly-skinned reptile sitting calmly on the floor beside my son.

As school cranked up again for the long run into Christmas, I wished we could have taken the lizard home with us. I thought things couldn't get any worse for Toby, but I began to be called in every day to appease him, to take him home, to sort out a problem, to apologise … It was sometimes very, very hard for me because these were my former colleagues I was talking to, and there was a relationship there that made things awkward. Sometimes I felt like I couldn't say the things I wanted to say, but equally I knew I needed to be Toby's advocate and speak up for him. It was so hard juggling it all, it was unbelievable. Neil was brilliant and often stepped in or spoke up when I felt I couldn't.

There were complaints from the other parents about our son. It was understandable, really; if I was worried about a child's behaviour in Ollie or Joe or Lauren's class, I would probably have said something too. But what was hard was that no one ever said it to my face. These were parents who, once upon a time, I might have been friendly with. I'd have felt so much better about it all if they'd just come up to me and said plainly, 'We have a real problem with your son.' I could have sat down and talked to them then; I could have explained. There was a real lack of understanding about autism, but no desire to learn more. A lot of the time, problems in the classroom *were* caused by Toby, but the teachers also said that he would get the blame for things even when he wasn't in school. It had got to the point where he was the naughty boy, and nothing we could do would change that.

On 12 December 2011, my phone rang as usual with a call from the school.

'Hello?' I said, wondering what the crisis was this time.

'Mrs Turner?' said the teacher. 'Can you please come in?'

It was oddly formal, but I thought no more of it and went into the school. Toby was at the end of whatever he'd done so I settled him down. The head teacher had asked to see me so I left Toby sitting on a chair outside his office and sat down opposite the principal, who was seated behind his desk.

'Mrs Turner, I'm afraid he's gone too far this time,' he said. And then he uttered the words I'd been dreading ever since Toby had started his education. 'We're going to have to exclude your son from school.'

12

A Memorable Winter

To be honest, I wasn't surprised. The tension this whole term had been escalating; there'd been a sense of a ticking time bomb and now the explosion I'd been anticipating had finally blown up in my face.

Toby was excluded for 'extreme behaviour which has escalated into physical and violent abuse directed at staff and pupils'. The principal told me the latest meltdown had climaxed with Toby scratching a computer screen with a pencil; the school equipment had been damaged.

He was excluded for one and a half days, and even though I'd seen it coming, it was absolutely gutting. The principal handed me a letter to take home:

I am writing to inform you of my decision to exclude Toby for violent behaviour in the classroom for a fixed period of one and a half days. This means he will not be allowed in school for this period. You have a duty to ensure that your child is not present in a public place in school hours. I must advise you that you may receive a penalty notice from the local

*authority if your child is present in a public place during
school hours …*

It was serious stuff. I collected Toby and took him home. He did
talk to me about what had happened, and as usual he felt very
guilty. Of the pencil and the screen he said: 'I didn't know it
would scratch, Mummy …'

As well as the exclusion, the head teacher had directed that
Toby would have to do jobs at home to pay for the screen.
I did understand that need, but I was also aware that what
was done was done. Best practice now shows that, when kids
with autism have misbehaved, what you need to do is repair
things as quickly as possible otherwise they latch onto the bad
behaviour and internalise the guilt to a level that affects their
health. I wanted Toby to be disciplined and for us then to
draw a line under it and finish it there and then – not let the
punishment carry on for weeks. But unfortunately the school
had other ideas, which was a shame, and I'm sure it didn't help
Toby. For, in time, he didn't connect the punishment with
the bad behaviour, but only with who he was; he thought he
was being punished for *being* Toby, and he already punished
himself enough for that.

After the exclusion period was over, Toby and I attended
a reintegration interview with the school. The teachers and I
explained to him why he hadn't been in school and what he
needed to do to ensure an exclusion didn't happen again. He
needed to use his words more to explain how he was feeling,
and to tell Miss Ellis when he felt anxious so that she could help
him before the meltdown went into overdrive. The school had

emotion colour cards available, and he was encouraged to make use of these.

To be honest, I think Toby seemed a bit bemused by it all. The meltdown for which he'd been excluded was a couple of days before by now; he could barely remember the violence with which he'd lashed out, or why he'd done it (if he could even remember the reason in the first place). All he heard in that meeting was simply more of what he heard every day.

There was one change we instigated following the exclusion, though: Toby went part-time. And you can guess who his teacher was going to be the rest of the time.

It really was just as well I'd given up my job.

Christmas 2011 was a non-excitable, nothing-to-see-here celebration. Toby had been excluded only days before the end of term, so we just did some Christmassy bits and pieces for the few mornings he was at home with me before the schools broke up. Lauren, for one, couldn't wait to see the back of school. She was having a tough time again, and had once more started counselling. That fragile family of mine seemed gossamer-thin.

While our festive celebrations were low-key, it was still a memorable winter – but for all the wrong reasons.

It happened one evening when I was sitting having tea with the kids. At least, I was having tea with Lauren and Joe and Ollie; Toby was refusing to eat. (Food was still a battleground from time to time … but then, almost *everything* in Toby's life was a battleground, to be honest.) The rule was that he had to sit at the table with everyone else and if he didn't want to eat then that was his choice (he would normally start eating after a while). He was using a very cross voice so I suggested that he went to his room to calm down. He'd taken so long arguing over his food that Lauren and Joe had already finished and got down from the table, but Ollie was still finishing off so I politely sat with him while Tobes stomped off upstairs.

Stomp, stomp, stomp … The familiar sound of Toby angrily plodding about his bedroom came through the ceiling; his room was right above the kitchen. And then everything went quiet. Worryingly quiet …

'Mum! *Mum*!' I heard Lauren calling from upstairs. 'Toby's trying to get out of his window!'

I ran up the stairs at breakneck pace and into Toby's room. He was standing on his bedside table, which was just beneath the window. His hand was on the window handle and he was rattling it in frustration, trying desperately to make the second-storey window open wide.

'Toby,' I said, very, very softly. He was so riled up, I didn't want my voice to add to his stress. I spoke only in a very gentle tone. 'What are you doing?'

'I want to jump out of the window,' he said. And then: 'I've had enough of this life!'

'Toby, you are sounding very cross.' *Stay calm*, I was telling myself inside, *stay calm. You can handle this, just talk him down.* 'Come on, down you get, let's sort this out.'

I edged towards him, and to my relief he climbed down willingly, putting his little hand in mine as he jumped off the table and down onto the carpet. I spent the next hour talking to him, 'debriefing' the episode, which is what we had to do after every explosion at school.

I wanted to kiss whoever had designed the windows. Thank God you had to press a button before they would open. For, without that safety feature, I was 100 per cent sure Toby would have carried out his death wish.

That incident was definitely a crying-in-the-shower moment. I felt worn down by everything, and so worried for Toby. He still hurt himself so often – nasty bruises and bites that would last for weeks, all along his arms. I simply didn't know what to do, how to make things better.

The other kids were affected by it too; of course they were. I had long conversations with some of them about it. Lauren, who had a very medical mind – she wanted to be a doctor when she grew up – found the lack of a cure for autism the most frustrating thing. It wasn't like any other illness, where you could just take a pill to make it better, or have an operation to excise the tumorous growth. But there was no quick fix, and no way of understanding it that would make it predictable and solvable. There was literally no way out, and it would last forever. To be honest, I think we all felt completely helpless about it.

As 'Supermum', though, I obviously couldn't admit to any such weakness at all. And so I reassured the kids that everything we were doing *was* helping Toby, even if it didn't always seem that way. There wasn't a cure, no, but we would sort it out *eventually*. As much for me as for them I clung onto that thought. I always used to say, 'By the time he gets to Year Six, we will have taught him all the things he needs to know that he can't do at the moment.'

Things such as how to join in our sarcastic family jokes. Despite our best attempts to teach him humour, he was still very wooden about it. On his best days, we would make a joke and tell him it was a gag, and he'd say, 'OK, it's a joke, I'm supposed to laugh now, aren't I? Ha, ha, ha …' On his worst days, he couldn't take the teasing and a light-hearted joke at a family dinner would cause a full-scale meltdown from Tobes.

But: 'By the time he gets to Year Six he'll understand …'

Year Six was four long and very hard years away, and at that moment I had no confidence at all we would even get there.

As the holidays wound down and the New Year drew near, I found myself watching telly one night: a rare moment of peace and quiet listening to the local evening news. And a feature came on about something called 'hearing dogs for the deaf'.

My first thought was that I was quite pleased the kids were in bed, because all the kids were dog-mad at that stage. They'd been going on and on and on about getting a dog, to the point where they'd even told Neil they would keep all of their Christmas money to save up to buy one. Neil, of course, had said, 'No, we're not having one.' How on earth would we cope with a dog as well as everything else? Life was hard enough as it was.

I watched the news story unfold, half my mind on that and the other half whirling away about how Toby would behave when he had to go back to school after the break, and how *I* would cope with having to home-school him. There was a child in the news piece: a deaf boy who found it hard to handle normal life. They showed how his specially trained dog helped him manage.

'Go and get Sam!' the child's mother instructed the dog. And this clever dog ran at a sensible pace up the stairs and gently tapped the deaf child on the hand so that Sam knew he now had to come downstairs because his mother wanted him. The dog could perform all sorts of tricks to keep the child safe, whether they were at home or out and about. I think they may even have shown Sam at the edge of a busy road, his dog in a high-vis jacket next to him, and how the dog sitting steadily on the pavement meant Sam didn't step out into the flow of cars. *That's what Toby needs*, I thought idly.

And then the newscaster went on to say that assistance dogs can help a multitude of people – *including children with autism …*

Oh. My. God.

With more energy than I'd had in months I got up from the sofa and got straight onto the computer to search for assistance-dog websites. I found a company called Dogs for the Disabled (now known as Dogs for Good). 'We're an innovative charity,' I read, 'exploring ways dogs can help people overcome specific challenges and enrich and improve lives and communities. Our assistance dogs support adults and children with a range of disabilities and also children with autism.' I clicked on the tab marked: 'Find out more'.

'An autism assistance dog gives the parent and child real independence, and provides a safer environment for the child so they feel more secure.' That was the key problem with Toby, I knew: he didn't feel safe, which was why he ran. Any one of us would do the same if we felt we were in danger. I couldn't stop thinking about how still and settled he'd become, sitting next to that lizard at Longleat Safari Park. Could an animal companion be the secret key to unlocking the puzzle of Toby Turner? I read on with growing excitement.

'The dog wears a special harness which connects it to both parent and child, and acts on instructions from the parent while the child is encouraged to walk alongside the dog. This offers greater independence to the child and parent, whilst ensuring the child is safe and unable to "bolt" if they become stressed or anxious. "Bolting" behaviour is also combated by training the assistance dog to automatically sit should the child attempt to run off.' I gave a wry smile; I could just imagine a big heffalump of a dog plonking himself down and aborting Toby's latest bid for 'freedom'.

'Having unlimited access to public places with the dog,' I read, 'enables the whole family to do simple things such as shopping, which may have been impossible before.'

Impossible – well, they were right about that. I clicked through more pages of the website. There were videos that showed what the dogs did and true-life testimonials of how they had helped families just like ours. I read and read and read all the stories and all the blogs, tears streaming down my face, because they were just lovely stories. And every single one of them had a happy ending.

As I read, I felt an unfamiliar sensation spreading inside me.

After a while, I realised it was hope.

I registered with the charity straight away. You had to fill in a form online about the problems that your child has, and it was a questionnaire that for once I felt happy about ticking off. Part of me realised that Toby's extreme needs were, in this instance at least, a positive thing. Hopefully they would put us straight to the top of the charity's list.

Neil, seeing my bright eyes and over-eager expression, advised caution. We always feel as a family that we don't run into luck and, while he was quick to acknowledge how amazing the dogs were when I showed him the videos, he also said, 'Yeah, but *we'll* never get one.'

'Well,' I said, 'we can try.'

When I next checked my emails, there was a message from the charity already waiting for me in my inbox. With trembling fingers, I double-clicked to open it up.

Dear Vikky, I read. *Thank you for your recent application to Dogs for the Disabled. Your responses suggest that you do fit our criteria.*

Yes!

However, our list is closed at the moment.

Oh no. I felt the disappointment settle around my shoulders like a cloak.

If you keep emailing us once a month to say that you're still interested, we will keep you up to date with our news and we can let you know when the list reopens in the future. Thank you for your interest in Dogs for the Disabled.

I was down, but I wasn't out; I made a note of the date. Every month, from then on in, I was going to email these people religiously. Nothing on this planet has more perseverance than the mother of an autistic child. They hadn't heard the last of the Turner family – not by a long shot.

13

The Only Way Is Up

The thought of an assistance dog was like a helium balloon: it bounced along beside me day by day, lifting my spirits up and never letting them sink – defying gravity. I tackled Toby's issues with a renewed vigour.

Continually reading my autism books as I was, I learned how lots of autistic children benefit from having a safe place, which is not very sensory-overloading. Toby had his own room, but of course it was filled with at least 600 boxes of brightly coloured Lego and 5,000 books on dinosaurs (his latest craze) and it had a border of red and blue space rockets on its cobalt walls, so it wasn't necessarily the most *calming* of places. Inspired by my books, I decided we would make him a safe space that was quiet and dark and peaceful.

There's a company called Izzy Whatnot and they make tenting that goes around a bottom bunkbed to make a kids' playhouse. So we got one of those in blue; it was like a garage and it had cars printed on it, and its own door. We attached it to the bed and left it at that: Toby needed it to be simple. I can still remember the first time we showed it to him. He said, 'Wow, that's amazing! I *love* it!'

He immediately dropped to his hands and knees and scrabbled into the tent and shut the door. 'It's so cool in here!' he exclaimed. 'I could bring my special box in here!'

There was a pause, and then he said, a moment later, 'It's a bit dark – could I have a light?'

And so I said of course he could, and we got him a torch to have in there, and he put his favourite dinosaur books and his favourite cushions from the playroom in there too. He loved those cushions. They were made of a cool crunchy cotton and Toby really enjoyed the *feel* of them. He used to fling himself down on the yellow cushions and he always said how much he liked the cool crispness of them. So I bought him a quilt cover in the same fabric. Although a nightmare to iron, it's worth it because Toby just adores it. It's blue with a racing car on the front, but the big selling point to Toby is its sensory feel.

The den started paying dividends almost straight away. I remember the first time he used it so clearly – I think he'd gone to his room to calm himself down after shouting at Ollie or Joe. I had popped my head round his door to check on him and my heart had dropped because he was nowhere to be seen. I couldn't see him anywhere and normally he would be sitting on the floor, listening to his audiobooks and it was just deadly quiet. I had this panic – *Oh my God, where's he gone? Has he jumped out of the window?* – and then there he was, within the safe confines of his den, lying with his thumb in his mouth on the crunchy cotton pillows.

It was just as well really that home was a sanctuary – because school sure as hell was *not*. Toby didn't want to go in at all after

Christmas. I would drive him in after lunch, all bubbled up with his audiobooks and his sunglasses, and drop him off in reception. When he realised what was happening, even though I'd explained it beforehand, he would literally cling to me, like a little monkey, but one who was screaming and crying with all his might. The staff actually had to prise him off me to get him to go in. It was so hard to go through. I'd just have to reassure him that I would be back and then I'd walk away: the most difficult steps for any mother to take.

That January Toby went through a series of assessments with different outreach services. One of the outreach staff commented that some of his anxiety was due to separation from me. And, I have to say, it was only me with whom he had that super-tight attachment; I was the only one who could calm him down. It made it difficult at times because, while Neil was fantastic with him, it was always me that Toby would call for and me that he wanted when he was upset. It meant Neil was unable to help me with the pressure of being Toby's go-to person. Always I had to be available for our son, at any moment of the day. I didn't mind, not one bit, but it was a huge responsibility.

The outreach teacher suggested that a 'communication diary', whereby I would write down what I was planning to do when I wasn't with Toby, would help my son settle down in school hours. The idea was that Toby could refer to it and it would help him to know what I was up to at any given moment. So I would write down hour by hour what I was going to do that day; I would also put notes in his snack box, saying I loved him, or just telling a joke that he could share with Miss Ellis that afternoon.

We tried so many tactics to help him through the school day, and the school were undoubtedly brilliant, I have to say, at responding to our ideas and coming up with ideas of their own. I cannot fault them on that at all.

Buoyed by the success of 'the den' at home, the school agreed to the creation of 'The Box'. It was just what it sounds like: a large cardboard box placed just outside his classroom as a 'safe place' for Toby to bolt to if he felt the need. When that wasn't effective, at Neil's suggestion they marked out with tape on the floor a space in the corridor, just down from the classroom, which was a 'zone' in which he could calm down. This worked well when he wasn't in heightened fight-or-flight mode, but nothing could stop him if he really wanted to run and hide. Then he would blast through anything and anyone who stood in his way.

Though Toby was only attending part-time, the hours he was in school were increasingly fractious and fraught. We had hoped the January assessments would lead to some proper, meaningful support, but after he had been through them all, we were told that he would receive only one-hour-per-week's support from the specially trained ILT (Independent Learning Tutor). It was the final straw. We could visibly see Toby being affected by the daily stress; to be honest, *we* weren't coping too well with it ourselves. On 1 February 2012, we wrote to his primary school and told them that we were temporarily removing our son from school. As we wrote in our letter, 'If the present arrangements are allowed to continue, we now see a significant probability of a serious incident occurring which causes injury to Toby, a member of your staff or another child.'

The plan was that we would try to reintroduce him to the school environment after lots of discussion and reviewing the options to ensure such a return was safe for everyone. In the meantime, I had full responsibility for my son's education.

Talk about pressure. The last thing Neil and I wanted was for Toby to fall behind educationally; he had enough struggles as it was. Equally, at that time he spent most of his hours at school hiding from the teachers or shouting at them, so he was getting nothing done there. I could only do my best, and so that's what I did.

It worked really well for Toby. He was obviously more relaxed in the home environment, but I was more relaxed about some of his behaviours too. So if he needed to have a wander around the room while he was thinking about a piece of work, that was fine; or if he needed to tap a pencil or chew something while he mulled over a maths problem, that wasn't an issue either.

Toby loved maths. He really likes playing with numbers. We'd run Ollie down to the pre-school in the car and I'd get Toby to practise his three times table for me on the journey there, and sound out his spellings on the way back. Once home, I'd settle him at the kitchen table and we'd try to do some work. I even managed to get him to do some written work, which at school they hadn't achieved for months. Toby was so self-critical, you see, that the moment his clumsy hand made a mistake with the pencil, even in mis-forming just one letter, his sense of failure would kick in and he'd kick off. But I used to say to him, 'It doesn't matter what your handwriting looks like, don't worry about that, let's just get it down on the page.'

It may also have helped that I had some bribes. We would sit there with some sweets, and every time he completed a whole sentence, he would have one. I remember he did a whole page of A4 writing one afternoon and I was so proud of him. It was a story about a dinosaur. I tried really hard to hang his learning on his passions, so for example, if we were going to do geography, I looked up lots of dinosaurs and noted down where their bones were found, and then we'd get a map and stick pins into the relevant spots. We did a lot of work on dinosaurs that spring!

But home-schooling couldn't be a long-term solution. I wasn't a qualified teacher, and Toby was entitled to his education from professionals, in a school environment where he could learn. There was no point in teaching him in an ivory tower at home, what would that teach him about life? And so about two weeks later, working closely with the school and the new ILT, a fabulous woman called Lorna, we slowly reintroduced Toby to school on a part-time timetable. He would attend in the mornings, and I would teach him work supplied by the school at our home in the afternoons.

Lorna was a very special woman. She was Toby's autism-specialist support worker. Following his assessments in January, she now came into the school once a week and dealt with the autism-specific side of things. She helped the school to work out how to handle Toby, and she helped Toby to work out how to deal with school. She wasn't a teacher, and she wasn't a TA who helped him with his work: she was a friend. She reminded me of a glass of pink champagne: she always wore brightly coloured tops, which flashed vividly beneath her very long blonde curly hair, and she just had this bubbly feeling about her.

Even with her expert help though, it was an uphill battle. Toby had meltdowns several times a day, despite his shortened timetable. A report from that period describes him hitting walls, throwing things, kicking off his shoes, destroying property, refusing to work, significantly disrupting classes, hitting out at people, running from classrooms and the school building and even trying to climb out of the school – he would literally scale the fences. All of us could see that his emotional outbursts were beginning more readily and escalating more quickly to challenging levels, while an outreach teacher wrote: 'His escapes have a dangerous quality to them as he will accidentally knock over smaller children and hide himself so staff do not know if he is safe.' The school were particularly worried because he'd slam doors when he ran away and they were concerned other children would get their fingers trapped and broken. Toby would be just like a bull in a china shop and he would slam the door, no matter who was nearby.

In March, Neil and I had to give formal consent that the school could physically restrain Toby if his unsafe behaviour warranted it. Oddly enough, signing our assent actually came as a bit of a relief. Before, if Toby had tried to climb the school fence to get out, the staff wouldn't have been allowed to lift him off and keep him within school grounds. Now, if he tried to get out of the building, they would have our blessing to stop him from doing so physically. Given Toby's lack of awareness at such times – he would happily have run straight onto a motorway without batting an eyelid when he bolted – it was actually safer to sign our names to the consent than not, and we trusted the staff implicitly.

Our consent came not a moment too soon. One morning, not long afterwards, Toby made a break for it. The school locked their gates during school hours but there was one gate that gave access to ambulances and things that had a gap of about a foot at the very bottom of it. On this particular bid for freedom, Toby had managed to get out of his class, out of the school, and was halfway under the gate before Miss Ellis caught up with him. Seeing him wriggling under the metal bars, moments from escaping into a busy town where he wouldn't have lasted two minutes by himself, Miss Ellis laid two strong no-nonsense hands on him and pulled him back. She was just in time.

After that incident, the school had to add special bolts to the gates to ensure Toby couldn't get out, and they added more metal to the bottom of that fence so his escape route was cut off. I remember the sound of a helicopter used to fill me with dread. I'd be waiting at home of a morning, both phones in my pocket, and that tell-tale beat of airborne blades would go over my house and I'd think, *He's got out. He's on the run.*

The helicopter never was coming for my son, but nine times out of ten when I went to pick him up, the only thing that had stopped him from running was that the school had been put into lockdown by their quick-thinking staff. Sometimes Toby did mornings with me and afternoons at school, and I can remember heading down to the school gates at 3 p.m. The gate normally opens dead on three o'clock, but time and again it would not open. All the other parents and I would be lined up, waiting. We'd all be thinking, *It's Toby …* And it always was.

I'd head to reception and the deputy head would be standing at the main double doors. Inside, there were two doors leading to different areas and each would be guarded by a member of staff. And Toby would be in reception, pacing in the corner, having a massive rant. I could hear him muttering under his breath, 'I'm going! I'm getting out of here. I hate this place, I'm going.' I was gutted that he was causing so much disruption, but my heart couldn't stop pounding in my chest as I witnessed his unutterably heartbreaking distress. When Toby is sad, he's not just sad, he's *distraught*. He feels everything so keenly and I, in turn, felt for him so much. I just wanted to nurture this little feral animal and make him feel better.

But nothing ever did make him feel better. Instead, his anxiety got worse and worse. More and more frequently, he would shout out in a pained voice, 'I want to kill myself!' The school caught him pressing metal keys against his throat; he hit himself over and over with a wooden saucepan he'd found somewhere. In his hands anything could become a weapon that he would turn on himself. It was just horrible for him; you could see that school was destroying him. It wasn't the school's fault, but it was difficult to blame Toby: he was only a child.

After school now it would take me three or four hours just to make him feel like he could be loved. He would go up to his room and I would follow him after a little while and then sit quietly in his room alongside him. After some minutes of silence, I would say, 'Would you like a hug?'

'No.'

I would keep on asking him.

'I don't deserve a hug, Mummy.'

Night after night he would sit in the corner of his room and say over and over that he didn't deserve to be loved and he didn't deserve to be cuddled because he was a bad person. He would only let me touch him, in the end, if he had his back to me and I was reaching out to him from behind, where he couldn't see me and the love that was in my eyes. I would gently stroke his back or play with his hair. Eventually, I might be permitted to wrap my arms around him, and I would wrap them really tight, and just rock backwards and forwards a little bit. Then I would start talking to him, little by little: reassuring words about how much he was loved and wanted and cared for. He was part of this family and nothing would ever, ever change that.

After a long, long while, he'd turn sideways. I could tell he'd warmed a bit by then and so we'd start chatting a little more. Finally, after hours of reassurance, he would come and give me a full tummy hug. At that point he always cried: an iceberg dissolving into salty tears. And oh, when he hugged me, he used to hug me with *everything* he had.

The time slots with the other children kind of went out of the window, though Neil picked up a lot of the slack. Toby's siblings really rallied round him, though. I could not have been prouder of them. Lauren, who had done a lot of work on her self-esteem in her own counselling sessions, spent a long time chatting with him about how to feel good about himself. She told me she found it heartbreaking to watch Toby being upset; that she just wanted to cry with him. But she was a brave girl and she'd often go in to see him without my knowledge because she wanted to make it better in any way she could.

If he'd had a bad day, I wouldn't go into detail, but I would tell the others, 'Toby's had a bad day today.' They would all go in, one by one, and have a chat and give him a hug. He spent most of his time upstairs, repairing from the damage that had been done.

In this way, we straggled and struggled to the end of Year Two. By the end of that academic year, the school and I had tried over forty different techniques to try to help Toby fit in and manage his school day. Amongst them was that he was now allowed to wear what he wanted to class because he found the uniform too much of a sensory overload and very uncomfortable. They said as long as he wore the school colours he could wear something else instead, so we got him some grey jogging bottoms and a soft white cotton T-shirt, and a navy-blue hoodie for the autumn term to come.

The autumn term … It almost didn't bear thinking about. But the only way was up, right?

Wrong.

14

This Isn't Working

It was a very quiet summer. Toby was a lot calmer, being out of school, but his flash-frights were still bubbling just beneath the surface and it no longer took much to set him off, and then the rest of the day would be ruined. We found we made very few plans; it simply wasn't worth it to try otherwise. It seemed best to stay at home and be neutral rather than try to have a good time and fail. For the harder I tried, the worse it seemed to go; the more ambitious we were, the more there was to go wrong.

I set my sights on simple family activities instead. *A pub meal*, I thought, *in a sunny beer garden, with a table in the shade for Tobes. What could go wrong with that?* But if the pub didn't have *exactly* what Toby wanted on the menu, there was no point in being there, because he wouldn't eat and he'd be really stroppy about it, and so I'd have to deal with him while Neil would be left to shepherd the other three kids: the family splintered, the way it always seemed to end up.

So I set my sights lower: a family walk in the woods. We didn't even take the whole family – just Ollie and Toby and Grandma and I went. We'd dropped Lauren off at a birthday party and I'd said jollily to the two younger boys, 'We'll just go and have a nice adventure in the woods!' I'd only planned to nip in for forty minutes or so, so I didn't take any snacks or water with me. Unfortunately, by my own admission I'm not the best at directions and we ended up getting a little lost for a while – maybe for another half an hour on top of the planned excursion. So we were walking round those woods for quite some time.

It was too much for Toby. At first, there were the usual complaints; the usual, sudden 'I'm thirsty!' (There was never any build-up to 'thirsty', it was always all-of-a-sudden, *bam*, 'I haven't drunk any water for three days and I'm on the cusp of death!' thirsty with Tobes.) I couldn't give him a drink, of course, because I didn't have anything on me, so I just tried to jolly him along while surreptitiously looking at the footpath signs for our car park.

Then he started getting tired. We'd been there for about forty minutes – the time I'd estimated in my head we would take – and Toby said abruptly, 'I can't walk any more, I can't go any further.' I tried to gee him along.

And then he realised we were lost – and that was just the worst thing. I honestly believe he thought he was going to die; I'm not joking. I remember we'd been in the woods for about an hour by then and he stopped by a tree with his arms folded and said, 'I'm not going any further! I'm dying! I need water!' People were going past, other families out for a stroll, and they must have been thinking, *What is she* doing *to that child?*

Again, I tried to cheer him out of it. 'It's OK, Tobes, we've found the way now, it's just a little bit further. Why don't we go and stand on that log for a bit of fun?'

But Toby wasn't having any of it. 'I'm going to die! I'm going to die!' he cried.

'Look, you can see the car park now, Tobes!' I said, pointing it out. 'It's just a little way now.'

Toby stomped to the car and flung himself in. 'I am NEVER doing that again!' he declared.

And he meant it. Family walks were now off the agenda. Whenever Neil or I or one of the other children suggested it, Toby would say, 'Well, we'll need to take a tent. And we'll need to take water. And we'll need to take snacks. And we'll need to take …'

'Toby,' I'd say, trying to make light of things, 'it's not a survival mission! We'll only be half an hour.'

But he wouldn't go unless we did as he asked … and so we just didn't go in the end.

What I found really sad was that Toby often knew the 'right' way to behave on days out and at activities, but he just found it really difficult to follow the 'normal' path that came so naturally to other children. It was like the 'true' path was north on a magnet, but Toby himself was due north too, and as hard as he tried to stick to the path he knew was right, something inside him was repelled by it and it pushed him away. For him, doing the 'right' thing was like fighting against a magnetic force that was urging him to go the other way. All too often, it was a battle he lost.

That year, Toby's friend Peter very kindly invited Toby to his seventh birthday party. I was very touched – Toby didn't get invited to many parties – and Toby was very excited. Peter has a lovely mum, Julie, who is the kind of unflappable woman who, if you turned up at her house with twenty kids in tow for tea, she'd simply welcome them in. Nothing seemed to faze her and nothing was ever too much trouble. I was worried about how Toby might behave – parties could be the worst kind of catalyst for his meltdowns – but Julie, in her understanding way, had simply said, 'We will make him feel comfortable.'

They did a truly wonderful job but, almost inevitably, it all went pear-shaped. The kids were playing with water-squirters and there weren't enough to go round. Toby had found it too difficult to share so he'd had a meltdown, tried to run out of the house and then barricaded himself in an upstairs bedroom. When I 'debriefed' the incident with him later that day, as I tucked him up in bed, he said quite honestly: 'I know I needed to share, Mummy, but I found it really difficult. I know it would have been better if I'd tried to join in, but I found it really hard.'

That was the very, very sad thing: he *knew*, he just couldn't do it. As he turned away from me that night, pulling his crunchy cotton duvet up over his ears as he rolled to face the wall, he said one final thing that broke my heart.

'I'll never be able to go to another party again,' he said. 'Nobody will *ever* want me there.'

With every disaster that unfolded, I had more reason than ever to keep on emailing the dog charity. Month after month that year, I sent them a message, diligently reminding them that we were still *very* interested in their assistance dogs – and month after month I received a reply to say that their list was still closed. By now that helium balloon of hope was starting to sag a little, looking droopy around the edges and hanging at mid-height, but I kept on emailing regardless. *Maybe one day …*

The only good thing about that summer for Tobes seemed to be the cooling fan we got him for his bedroom. It was a stupendously hot summer so we'd got all the kids fans for their rooms; Toby, with his sensitivity to heat, seemed to love his the most. We were always looking for things that would help him to sleep better, and sleep through the night, and in the fan we'd stumbled on a good one. We used to find him lying on the floor right in front of it; he'd take all the covers off his bed and sleep on the carpet next to the fan because he liked it so much. He had it on every night.

When the weather started to cool at the start of September and the nights turned chilly, we put the fans in the attic. Toby came to me the morning after they'd disappeared and said that he couldn't sleep without the sound; it turned out it wasn't just the cool air he liked, it was that soothing white noise that the whirr of the blades had made.

'Well,' I said, 'why don't we see if we can find that sound for you?'

So Toby and I sat and listened to all the different 'white sounds' noises you can get on iTunes. He would listen hard and say, 'That's not right' and 'That's not the one.' But then we hit on the fan-oven sound effect, and like Cinderella and her shoe, it was a perfect fit. I downloaded it and put it on his iPod, and that night we played it for him as he went to sleep.

'Ah,' he said happily. 'That's *much* better.'

He breathed a sigh of relief. It was so lovely for me to have made life more comfortable for him.

I knew he would need all the help he could get now that school was starting again.

* * *

From the very start, Year Three for Toby had, ominously, a lot of changes for him to contend with. Firstly, he had a new TA who would be job-sharing with Miss Ellis a couple of days a week; her name was Anna. Another change was that Toby's classroom was now in a mobile unit, rather than in the main school building. Now, that was a problem. The classrooms had been hard enough for him to bear, but now the room he was in was even smaller, and even more echoing, and even more tightly packed with other humans with their loud voices and commands and irritations. Worst of all, it was stuck out on a limb next to the playground, separate to the main school. There was no Box right next door to hide in; no 'safe zone' marked out in a nearby corridor for him to run to. There wasn't even a spare table he could hide under, or a cupboard he could sneak inside: there was nowhere to go.

As before, the school tried their best to help. They made a workspace for him outside one of the classrooms, but it was in the main school corridor. It was very exposed and people were always walking up and down. Toby just needed a nook or cranny to feel safe in so he could calm down, but there was nothing like that. The school had a new 'chill-out' room, a kind of snug, which had a sofa and games and some work tables in it; it was mostly used for after-school activities. Sometimes Toby could work in there, but not always, and the times it was booked out or when he was not permitted to use it were always very frustrating for him.

So Toby found his own 'safe space'. When it all got too much for him, he would run out of the mobile classroom, across the playground and halfway down the main corridor, to where this little art cupboard was located. It was crammed with supplies, but it was dark and discreet and it gave him a safe place to calm down, where he could shut out the rest of the sensory world while he returned to his own senses.

He spent an awful lot of time in that art cupboard.

He was still only doing part-time. Basically, what happened was he'd go to school in the morning, where he spent most of the session hiding in the cupboard, and then I'd be given all the work he didn't do to complete with him in the afternoon. As before, at home, he would generally do the work OK, assuming he wasn't worn out or nauseous from the morning's various trials and tribulations.

It was so obvious that the school wasn't working for him that Neil and I, time and again, pushed for the statement of special educational needs that would allow Toby a place at a specialist autism school. But the paperwork and assessments seemed to be taking forever. All of us – Toby, Neil and I, and the school – were stuck with what he had. We all tried to make the best of it.

Some days, it worked well. Toby was particularly fond of Miss Ellis and would greet her with a hug and be very chatty. With both the TAs' help, he would have days that, when I picked him up, he described as 'great!' I helped him as much as I could and would often stay for some of the school day to help him remain calm, joining him for a movement class or something like that. At times, he could be enthusiastic, diligent, hard working, well mannered …

But those were the exceptions to the rule. More often, Miss Ellis or Anna, or the SENCO Pam would have to take me to one side when I picked him up to give me a concerning report. They told me of Toby repeatedly trying to harm himself, swearing, breaking things, declaring that he wanted to die, pushing or smacking people.

I myself saw him demonstrating behaviour that he never displayed at home, where normally countdowns and warnings elicited eventual good behaviour. Time and again I had to discipline him or impose sanctions such as no Internet or removing his DS because he refused to follow the rules. Some rules were new to him and had to be taught: he'd started up a new habit of poking other children in the back of the neck with various long thin objects, and I had to explain that the neck was a very vulnerable place and his actions might make people feel frightened. Toby had explained he hadn't wanted to make them feel that way at all; he was only copying Harry Potter with his wand. We had to be very, very careful what Toby watched and listened to because he would copy anything he saw.

His behaviour spilled over into our weekends too. We never planned to do anything, so we were usually all cooped up inside. There were incidents of Toby hitting his sister intentionally; of him accidentally hurting his brother and then feeling so guilty that he threatened to kill himself and once again tried to jump out of his bedroom window. He was out of control.

The stress and pressure started to make him very unwell. He was just so tense, *all* the time. He was waking every night, sleepwalking down the stairs in distress. Almost every day, he would say he felt poorly, and often he would be physically sick or have diarrhoea. Perhaps as a consequence, he refused his food, and the weight started to drop off him again. He looked pale and sickly, with dark circles under his lovely green eyes. To my horror, those shadows matched the bruises on his arms. Toby was struggling so much that his self-harming had now reached epic proportions. He would have bite marks that lasted weeks, going through the whole bruising process. Always he was trying to punish himself for what he'd done and how bad he was. It was horrible. It was really *really* horrible for him – and for me, to watch: because he was *suffering*. And you never want your child to suffer, do you? He just kept on saying, constantly, 'I am going to kill myself.'

I wanted to run away with him. There were times when he would be in bed at night, and he'd be really peaceful, and I would just think, *Perhaps if we both died, we could go and be together and get away from all this …*

It was never seriously thought through – I mean, I would never do it. I never thought about doing it, not with any plan in mind or anything like that. But the situation was just so appalling, so very overwhelming. I'd look at this little baby in the bed, who was just peaceful – for *once*; and sometimes it was the *only* time he was peaceful … Oh, it was horrible. It was so hard.

I wanted desperately to run away. I wanted to say to Neil and all the kids, 'Come on, let's get in the car, all of us, and just go. I don't care where, let's just go, let's just get away from it all …'

But there was nowhere to run to. And what we were running from, we would be taking with us. It was an impossible situation, without an end in sight.

Understandably, the pressure on both Neil and me was intense. We never argued, but we had no time together at all. Constantly tired and stressed, I would generally be in bed by 8 p.m., knowing Toby was going to have a disturbed night. I can remember crying in bed some nights, just thinking, *Where is all this going? How on earth am I going to make it better?*

If Neil and I did get some time alone in the evening after the children had gone to bed we would just talk over the day's events (mainly around Toby) and plan the next day – who was going to do which lift, attend which meeting, support the other children. We couldn't leave Toby with anyone, of course, so either Neil and I would split up or we would take Toby with us – including to the other children's parents' evenings. We were co-operating with each other, each playing our part in the mechanical team that ran our family, but we didn't really seem like husband and wife anymore.

But my major concern was of course Toby. Over that term things got worse and worse and worse. It got to the point where we felt, if it wasn't school we were sending him to, what we were doing would be deemed abusive. We could see him losing weight; we could see him being stressed. He was sick most of the time because of the anxiety. And we were worried for his safety every time he was in school because we knew all he wanted to do was run home.

In November 2012, Toby was excluded again. While I understood the decision, I felt frustrated with the education system: it wasn't what he needed. But the worst thing of all was that he was excluded for 'attacking' Anna, and as a result she withdrew from being his TA. I think she'd been finding him difficult anyway – he *was* a very difficult child. On this occasion Toby had been refusing to do a piece of written work and he had run off to the art cupboard. I only have his version of events, but Toby had grabbed a bamboo stick that was part of the supplies in the cupboard and he had poked her with it. For her it was the final straw, I think.

My take on the situation was that never, in a million days, no matter how bad it got, would I give up on a child – but then again, Toby is my child and not hers. I can also understand that he had physically hurt her and that all this had been building up over a very long time.

Without Anna's support available any more, Lorna, Toby's ILT, was drafted in to be his replacement TA. You would think, given Toby liked Lorna, that this would be a good thing. But Toby knew Lorna as a friend, a support, someone who was a pal. She wasn't someone who asked him to do work – but now she was. It was a change in their relationship, and we all knew how Toby felt about change …

About two weeks after Toby's second exclusion, when he was back at school, Neil and I walked the familiar route into the building. It was right at the start of December. For once, we weren't there to discuss Toby's needs, but to support Ollie, who was being a fabulous all-singing, all-dancing reindeer in his first-ever nativity play with the reception class. He was so excited about us coming to see him, bless him. Ollie was a real performer – the entertainer of the family. He loved music and dancing and he was quite a drama queen, so this stage debut was of the utmost importance. Neil and I couldn't wait to see him strut his stuff.

We took our seats in the hall and the children edged nervously onto the stage (all except Ollie, who couldn't wait to step into the limelight). Ollie looked so cute in his outfit: he had brown antlers and a proper little reindeer suit with a big fat tummy. As the pianist started to play the melody, though, I became aware that the door at the back of the hall was opening. Someone I recognised came in. It was Lorna. She caught my eye and mouthed at me: 'I need you to come out.'

Trying not to obscure the view of any parents, I stood up and walked out. I had to turn my back on Ollie and step out into the corridor. I knew, of course, what the problem was.

'He's in the snug,' said Lorna.

I went straight there and looked through the window. It was clear that Toby had lost it. At that stage, he was just sat on the yellow sofa with his thumb in his mouth – but all around him was complete devastation. He had wrecked the room. He'd tipped out boxes of cars and Lego and pencils. He'd flung about all the school's puzzles; the pieces were jumbled together on the floor. The tables and chairs were all upended; he had hurled all of the furniture about. Everywhere you looked, there was mess and destruction.

I went in slowly and gave him a hug, and we just sat there for ages, cuddling. Then I said, as brightly as I could manage, 'Come on, Tobes, let's tidy all this up.'

We cleaned up the mess and after a while Lorna came in to help us. She was the most understanding woman. And I said to her, 'This isn't working.'

She gave me such a warm smile, to show me how much she cared. 'No,' she said honestly, 'it's not.'

And at that point I decided: *Enough is enough*. We couldn't do it to him anymore. It was almost like a stamp: FINISHED. We are done. By this time the play was over and Neil came to join me. We decided together: our son is not going back to school.

Toby was excluded, of course, but it didn't really make a difference – he was never stepping foot in that building again. The staff, as ever, were amazing. Conscious that I had missed out on Ollie's play because of Toby's upset, they rallied round and told me they were going to get me in to the second performance, which was later that day. I didn't have a ticket, I didn't have anything, but they gave me a seat right on the front row, with a perfect view of my youngest little boy, and that was so lovely of them. Everybody there was just so determined to get me into the show, so I didn't miss out on Ollie's moment of glory.

The pianist started up the melody, and this time there were no interruptions. I watched as Ollie pranced onto the stage and proudly belted out his best version of 'Rudolph, The Red-Nosed Reindeer'. And I couldn't stop the tears that streamed down my face. I just sat and cried through the whole thing. With pride, with relief – with uncertainty. I had no idea what the future would hold.

And I would never have guessed the twist in the road that was coming for us. Because, that same Christmas, I received an email from the dog charity. I opened it wearily, expecting the usual response: *We regret to inform you that our list is still closed …* My helium balloon was right out of air and lying in a raggedy heap on the floor, limp and lost and forgotten.

But this time the email said: *We would like to invite you to an open day to learn more about our work …*

The Christmas song that was playing on the radio said it all: *Hallelujah.*

15

Magical Dogs

Neil looked after the kids while I attended the open afternoon. It was held at the charity's headquarters. I had no idea what to expect as I headed into the reception, but I couldn't stop the irrepressible excitement that was fizzing in my stomach.

There were about ten or eleven other people there, all of them with their own stories of living with an autistic child; all of us desperate for the kind of miraculous help the assistance dogs could provide.

I can remember that place so clearly. We had to walk back outside to get to the room the information day was being held in, and the route took us past the dogs' kennels. The HQ was where the dogs lived, you see, while they were in training. There were dogs coming out all over the place – big ones and little ones and white and brown and yellow ones, ones with black patches and ones with white spots. There were all shapes and sizes and breeds, a real mishmash of dogkind. They weren't noisy or barking: they were just wandering around obediently with their trainers. The place was a hive of activity, but it had this wonderful calmness about it. Everyone was focused on their dogs, and we actually saw some training going on as we walked. A door would open and a dog would trot through and sit down on command, and then receive a treat. Then the trainer would summon him back and the door would close and then they'd repeat the whole thing all over again. There was a really soothing rhythm to it all and the whole atmosphere was quite magical.

Oh dear, I thought. *I've only just got here and already I want to cry ...*

I felt so emotional. Part of it, I'm sure, was the horrendous stress we had just gone through with Toby. Part of it was relief to be attending this day at last, to have hope again that something might come of it. But another part of it was simply being there, in this place where dogs were trained to help children, and every single one of them looked proud and happy and simply very, very jolly to be doing so. It was a positive, calm environment, and I realised it had been a very long time since I'd been in one of those.

We were ushered into a bright room with a big bi-folded door that opened right out. There was a large screen in front of us, on which, later, they'd show us some videos of the dogs. But first we got to meet Kelly, who was the autism team's trainer and who would be our main point of contact with the charity. She was leading the information day.

I could tell straight away that she was a really nice person. She was a short woman with dark shoulder-length hair and she was simply very warm in her manner. What I loved is that you could tell from her opening speech that she knew *exactly* what we were all going through. She had this sincere heart in her that really understood what it was like to be a family living with autism.

For so long I'd been banging up against people who didn't have that knowledge and simply didn't understand Toby's condition, but here everybody understood – and wanted to help.

Kelly gave a short presentation about how the dogs worked. She stressed how giving the animals were and the difference they made. I just wanted to sit and cry constantly, the whole way through, it all sounded so lovely! They showed us some videos of the dogs at work and then Kelly said, 'We'd like to introduce you now to two very special dogs who have already been matched with families, to show you some of the skills they have.'

We all sat up at that point, craning to see. And in padded the stars of the show. There was a dog who I think was possibly a Poodle crossed with a Retriever, who was just the curliest-furred little thing you can imagine. She was called Fizz. With her was Ollie, a huge handsome golden Labrador. Both of them were super-alert and clearly very clever, and there was a kind of pride in the way they performed their skills and tricks. *Very impressive, isn't it?* Ollie seemed to say with a roll of his big brown eyes. *Bet you've never seen* that *before*, declared Fizz with a shimmy of her curly-wurly tail.

Kelly put them through their paces. I remember her popping a sticker on her leg and saying, 'Touch,' and Ollie dabbing it gently with his wet black nose. That skill was one where, if your child was doing a behaviour that you didn't want, the dog could nudge the child and the child would know to stop – without your having to tell them off and the situation having the potential to escalate. There were all sorts of things the dogs could do. They could learn to have their foot measured in the shoe-shop machines so that their child would follow their lead in obediently doing the same (*sounds like a good one*, I thought …). You could get them to spin round in a circle on command as a distraction technique. The basic training for autism is that they wear a jacket that has two leads on it: one goes around the child's waist and the other is held by the parent. The dogs are then taught things such as to sit at the kerb, and even if the child moves, they don't move. And if the child goes to run, they're taught to stand really still and not move, because that then stops the child from running away. You can get them to head-rest on your lap, which is a calming ploy, and you can even train them to sit safely across a child, putting all their weight on them, in a kind of deep pressure or deep massage that many autistic kids find comforting and secure. It was all incredibly impressive and hope-giving. I felt those tears again, pricking at the backs of my eyes, but they were such happy tears. It all sounded so amazing.

Kelly made sure to say that at the end of the day they were just dogs and they still needed a doggy life alongside their work, but you could tell she loved showing them off too. She told us that, if any of us had a specific problem that the dog would need special training to combat, that could easily be arranged. They pair the dog to the child and so they can train the animals to help with the specific difficulties of that particular child, whatever they may be.

Kelly was witty, as well as matter-of-fact. She added with a smile, 'But, you know, if you want the dog to hang the washing out, well, I'm afraid it's not going to do *that* …'

At the end, there was an opportunity to ask questions. Though I knew the Labrador Ollie was going to a different home, it made me wonder what would have happened if he'd been *our* dog, given we already had an Ollie at home of the all-singing, all-dancing reindeer-impersonating type.

I stuck up my hand and asked, 'How do you get on if there's a child called Ollie and the dog's called Ollie?'

Kelly said with a smile, 'It's the luck of the draw!'

The dogs are named by litter, and each litter is allocated a different letter of the alphabet; so, for example, Ollie obviously arrived in the 'O' litter. Sometimes, the dogs are named by the charity's sponsors too.

Neil had charged me with a question before I left for the day, so I stuck my hand up to ask that. 'Um, can you take the dogs on holiday with you?' I paused. 'To France?' (Neil and his three weeks away *en vacances* were untouchable necessities.)

'Oh yes,' said Kelly, 'just not in the first year. We like to get them settled first, before you start taking them to a foreign country.'

'OK,' I said, smiling and nodding. That would be music to Neil's ears. I felt the need to cry all over again.

Then someone voiced the question that we were all thinking but nobody had yet had the courage to ask. 'So … how do you *get* one of these magical dogs?' he said.

'Well,' said Kelly, 'there's not a waiting list as such. It's whether the right dog for you comes up. We match the dog to the child. We will give you all an application form this afternoon, which will ask you questions about your child and your family set-up and what kind of help you need, and then we pair the dog to your child based on personality, the dog's skills, and what that dog can cope with. It's a very strong matching process.'

Everyone was nodding enthusiastically, and Kelly started handing out the application packs for us to take home. There was a real buzz of anticipation; it had been such a lovely, lovely day. I couldn't wait to get home and tell the family about it.

Another member of our group stuck her hand up. 'Um, I know you said there isn't a waiting list,' she began, 'but how long *is* the wait?'

'It really varies,' said Kelly sympathetically. As I say, she genuinely understood the pressure we were all under, all of us parents who had managed to get a day away from our autistic children for this very important session. But though she was sympathetic, all the sympathy in the world couldn't soften the bite of what was to come. She continued: 'It can be a two-year wait.'

Two years ... Sometimes it was hard enough to live through two minutes with Toby at his worst. Nevertheless, buoyed up by the day's events and my memories of the skills of the wonderful Ollie and Fizz, I headed home clutching my application pack, feeling a lot more relaxed than I had done when I'd headed out that morning. Something about being with those dogs just made me feel calm. It was incredible, the power they had.

When I got home, I told the whole family all about my exciting day out. I said how wonderful the place was and I told them in great detail about the remarkable Ollie and Fizz. The human Ollie thought it was very funny indeed that the dog had the same name as him. All the kids were hanging onto my every word; they were still major activists for the 'let's get a dog' campaign and this was a boon to their crusade that they had never anticipated. I told them cautiously that we were going to try to see if we could get one of these very special dogs, but there were no guarantees. Although I tried a little bit to dampen their enthusiasm, it was very hard when all I wanted to do was jump on their bandwagon like Boudicca at her best.

That same night, Neil and I pored over the paperwork and very quickly returned the completed form to the charity. Now, it was a waiting game. We could only hope that we would be one of the lucky ones. Two years seemed an awfully long way off in the future …

In the meantime, my primary concern was Toby's educational future. Having withdrawn him from school, and with no place at any other establishment ready for him (Neil and I were hoping against hope that one would become available soon), I felt it was up to me to deliver what he needed. I did have a lot of support from Lorna, who was absolutely brilliant. Toby's former school, too, still provided us with some work, and we were offered this empty classroom in Banbury where Lorna and I could teach him, so we would go there and do his work. To be honest, I don't know why we couldn't do it at home, because it was absolutely exhausting going up and down to Banbury all the time, especially because the other kids still needed picking up in Bicester and looking after there; nevertheless, at least a space was provided. We also went to the Hub in Bicester, which is like a youth centre; they had a craft room where we could do art projects (a.k.a. draw pictures of dinosaurs).

In some ways, I would have preferred it if I could have done the home-schooling completely independently, because I would have done things a bit differently and taught him more out in the open and things like that, rather than being stuck in a classroom all day long doing dry old worksheets. The pressure of doing the schoolwork was really hard, on both of us. Nonetheless, I knew it was the right thing to have done, to have got Toby out of that ever more difficult environment, so I simply put my head down and battled on.

Toby, it's fair to say, was definitely a happier bunny now. He had been at rock bottom before, but now he seemed more settled and had far fewer meltdowns. I was so relieved to see an improvement in his self-harming, and he declared much less often that he wanted to kill himself. Yet this only came after a huge amount of reassurance from me that he wasn't a bad person and that the school hadn't been the right school for him, rather than him not being the right person for the school. During the day I spent hours building his confidence up and showing him that he was an amazing little eight-year-old boy.

At that point, he'd built up such a relationship with me that, as long as I was by his side, everything was pretty much OK. In the last few months at school, in fact, he'd developed this crushing concern for my safety, so that he'd panic and cry if I so much as walked round the car in the car park, for fear that I was about to be run over. If we were at my mum's together and I just nipped to the loo, within seconds he would kick off because he couldn't see me, even though he was really calm immediately beforehand.

It was a huge responsibility. A lot of the time it did feel too much for me alone to take. It was really, really difficult. I tried to balance it, but I also worried constantly whether I was handling it all in the right way. *Am I doing the right thing?* I wondered. *Am*

I *the right thing? Just because he relies on me, it doesn't necessarily mean that I'm doing right by him …*

Toby accompanied me everywhere. He joined me on all the school runs, buttoned up in his winter coat with his shades on and his audiobooks playing in his ears. When it was just him and me in the car, he would take off his headphones and he would sit at the side of me and we would chat and put the world to rights. It was quite a drive to Banbury so on the way we would point things out to each other on the journey and have a long old natter. Then when we got there, we would get out and I would do his work with him and then we'd drive back and pick up Ollie and drive home and I'd start preparing Toby's schoolwork for the next day and reviewing what he'd achieved, and I'd sort out the other kids and try to think about dinner …

It was a lot to do and I found it very hard. Normally, I'm quite organised, but it felt like all that just went out the window: it was just so very busy. It was a huge, huge pressure and extremely time-consuming; as a mum of four so often I just wanted to have five minutes' peace to do a load of washing … It was exhausting. The tutoring alone was a full-time job, but there was so much else to think about, too. So often I felt like someone had turned a tap on in my foot and just drained everything, drained it all out of me. Most days, by early evening I felt so exhausted that I couldn't even hold a conversation. It was overwhelming, but I just kept telling myself, *This is what you've been dealt, you just need to get on with it. Pull yourself together, woman!*

I never felt fully in control of everything – or anything. Always I seemed to be darting across the county all the time, here, there and everywhere, and there was never a moment to myself, for Neil or sometimes even for the other children. Lauren had a school show on around that time and I insisted we went to that; Toby came with us in his ear defenders and sat through the whole of *We Will Rock You*. Actually, he thought it was the best thing ever.

I tried to make life as normal as possible for the rest of the family, but I'm sure they noticed the wheels were coming off the cart. Often I'd say, 'You know what, kids, we've got nothing in for dinner but we'll sort it out!' Before, I'd always cooked meals from scratch; now, takeaways started creeping in. The washing piled up in the laundry bins; the dust accumulated on the mantels. For someone as house-proud as me, it was a disaster. If I'd had another toddler around the house at that time, 'Hoover' would definitely *not* have been their first word! Things were slipping, and while the house had always been busy in the past, before it had been controlled chaos. Now, things were out of control.

At night, I was so, so tired. There weren't enough hours in the day to do everything. I was so tired that I needed to go to bed, but I also knew I had to get up early to do this and that, and the thought of everything I had to get done piled up in a suffocating mass. I just felt overwhelmed. Toby was still up in the night; he'd never slept well. He would always come and find me. Sometimes it was just to say, 'I love you, Mummy.' Sometimes I think he was just checking I was still there.

We went on like this for a few months, just about keeping our heads above water. And then one day the phone rang. I grabbed it from where it was nestled between Ollie's overflowing school bag and a pile of unmatched socks and answered breathlessly, 'Hello?'

'Hello there,' the vaguely familiar voice on the end of the line said. 'It's Kelly from Dogs for the Disabled. Would it be OK if I came for a home visit to discuss your application for a dog?'

I couldn't say 'yes' fast enough.

16

One Very Special Dog

Ding dong!

There was a sound like thunderclaps on a mountain as the children raced from all four corners of the house to converge on the front door. I fought my way through them, laughing.

'Come on now, kids, give her some room,' I said. I couldn't help the smile that was spreading across my face. We were all so excited about Kelly's visit. 'Hello again,' I said cheerily, as I opened the door wide.

Kelly stood on the doorstep, a beaming smile on her lips. She'd brought a colleague with her, a woman in her late twenties who, it turned out, was being trained up. She had short spiky hair and was very quiet.

'Come on in,' I said.

We all convened in the kitchen. Neil popped the kettle on and we sat round the table as a family for a chat. Toby hovered, looking with interest at the strangers in our midst.

'Hello, I'm Toby,' he said, announcing himself. He stood for a bit and then said, 'Can I go now?'

Kelly smiled at him. 'Of course you can,' she replied, and he scampered off upstairs to play in his bedroom on his own.

The other kids stayed with us at the table. The meeting was, we assumed, the next stage in the application process – and indeed, Kelly quickly reached into her bag and brought out yet another questionnaire that she filled in as we talked. She wanted to know more about what we were looking for in a dog and the kind of help we needed.

'Are there any behaviours Toby does that you'd like to stop?' she queried.

'Not exactly,' Neil replied. 'He flaps a lot, but if he needs to have a flap, he needs to have a flap; that really doesn't bother us. He does bolt, though, and run off. We would like some help with that.'

I piped up. 'We would like him to have a companion,' I said, 'someone who makes him feel safe.'

A friend, in other words.

'OK,' said Kelly. 'So perhaps a dog who can retrieve a toy, so that Toby could interact with him like that?'

We nodded. I could just picture Toby out in the garden, shades on, throwing a ball for his very own pet dog.

'How about football?' Kelly asked. I think all the kids' eyes goggled. 'Some families would like their dog to play football.'

'Um, that's OK,' I said, giggling a bit. 'Toby's not a massive fan of football.'

'And what about you as a family?' she asked next. 'Are there days out, places you'd like to go?'

I could feel the children kind of still beside me. I'm sure Lauren and Joe could remember those crazy half-term holidays where we used to go out on an adventure every day of the week, but it had been a long, long time since we'd even *tried* to go anywhere. I don't think we'd realised consciously it had happened, but we never went out as a family any more. It was always too much like hard work. We had just stopped; we no longer bothered. It caused more upset to everyone to try than not.

It was hard to read the emotions on their faces as Kelly asked the question, but I think it would be fair to say they were upset and disappointed that our escapades had come to an end. As for Ollie, he didn't have any memories of anything different; he had missed out completely on the times that had made Lauren and Joe as people.

'Well …' I said. 'I'm not sure where we would want to go.'

We were so shut down to places we could go, I didn't even know what to ask for.

Kelly continued with her questions and suggestions. She listed a whole lot of things that the dogs could do and we'd say, 'Oh, that would be useful,' and 'Yes, that would be OK.' The big thing for us was the social interaction and the idea of Toby having a friend. I thought of what a difference it would make to me, if he had a friend. A dog could well share some of the responsibility I had in looking after him, if we were both his number-one fans. We would be part of the same team.

Kelly then raised the logistics of having a dog in the house. There were changes that would need to be made to accommodate the assistance dog, she said. We'd have to create a special dog toilet space out in the garden, and we had to buy a stairgate so that we could designate a safe area in the house for the dog – so that, if Toby ever got violent (which some autistic children do), the dog would be protected.

After a while, as we adults talked and talked and talked, Ollie got down from the table and went off to play, but the older two stayed around for most of Kelly's visit. They were both really, really excited about the idea of getting a dog. Lauren was in Year Eleven by then, about to take her GCSE exams, and I think it was a welcome distraction from all the pressure she was under academically.

Toby would pop down now and again as the meeting continued. 'Are you going soon?' he asked Kelly bluntly.

We all smiled to ourselves. 'He's not trying to throw you out,' I said, 'he's just had enough of you being here.'

'I won't be much longer now,' she said. 'In fact, I've just got one more thing to do. I hope it's OK, but I've brought a dog with me. I'd like to bring him in so that you can get a feel for what a dog is like in your house. You might find that he takes up a lot of room, or it's not for you. Would that be OK?'

'Yes!' cried Lauren and Joe together, before Neil or I could even speak. I don't think they could wait to meet him.

'So this dog,' said Kelly, 'is about one and a half years old. He came to us from the Irish Guide Dogs, along with his sister Shannon. Like all our dogs, he went to puppy socialisers for the first year of his life, and he's recently started his kennel training, which is much more advanced. There are obviously lots of areas our working dogs can head into, but this particular dog is very assertive, which makes him perfect for the autism training.'

'Why's that?' I asked.

'Well, autism assistance dogs need to have that firm confidence about them. At work, they'll have a child pulling in one direction and their handler will say, "Stay where you are," so they need to be able to stick to their guns and not respond to the child.

'Now, he's very big. Are you sure you're happy for me to bring him in?'

How big can a dog be? I thought. 'Sure!'

Kelly and her colleague got up from the kitchen table and headed outside to where the dog was waiting.

'Kids!' I called. 'The dog's coming in now!' There was another round of thunderclaps as they powered down the stairs and all gathered excitedly in the family room. 'Now remember,' I said to them all, 'this isn't going to be *our* dog. Kelly is just letting us see what it would be like to have a dog. OK?'

'OK, Mum,' they chorused.

We all heard the handle on the front door move, and then we heard the tell-tale *click-clack* of a dog's claws on our wooden floor. *A dog was in the house!*

And then Kelly came into the living room with the most enormous dog I had ever seen in my life. He was *tall* – there was no other way to describe it. A Labrador Retriever Cross, he was about 70 centimetres high and over a metre long. I swear there may have been a bit of Irish Wolfhound in there too as he was just huge. He had a glossy, plain black coat and bright brown eyes and floppy black ears. He was a bit boundy, and you could tell he was a young dog; it almost seemed like he was testing out his long legs as he came bouncing into the lounge, sniffing away as he took in all the enthralling scents of this unfamiliar home.

The children and Neil and I crowed as one, 'Oh, he's *lovely*!'

I had rarely, if ever, seen Toby as excited. He started talking very quickly, very fast, about how very lovely the dog was, and he was running his hands all over the dog's inky fur, talking nineteen to the dozen. The dog stood there calmly, very chilled, not at all perturbed by the exhilaration he had created in the entire family with his appearance, nor by Toby's ever-stroking hands.

'Why don't you give him a treat, Toby?' Kelly asked. She gave all the children some dog treats and told them they could ask the dog to sit and stay and lie down. They gathered in a circle around the dog and Toby began by shouting out his command.

'Sit!' he cried.

The dog graciously bent his long back legs and seated his black hairy bottom on the cream carpet.

'Good boy!' Toby gave him a cuddle and a treat. 'Lie down!' he said next.

The dog stretched out his elongated front legs as though relaxing on a sun lounger, and plonked his whole body weight on the floor. He gave a sigh as he landed, which covered Toby's face in doggy breath. Toby giggled at the sensation. 'Good boy!' Another treat was dished out.

It was so lovely to see Toby so interactive. After a while, it became clear that he wanted most of the dog's time so we had to say to him, 'Why don't you let Ollie have a turn now, Tobes? It can be Ollie's turn, then Toby's turn; then Lauren's turn, then Toby's turn. OK?'

'OK!' said Toby happily. He was fine with it.

And so all the children took it in turns to shout their commands and distribute the treats. The dog obeyed all of them to the letter, joyfully and with good grace; he was so well trained. He did everything, just as they said. The kids were playing with him constantly, and it just went on for ages and ages and ages. It was so heart-warming – there's no other word for it; it literally warmed my heart – to see the children's excitement.

Being a cautious mum, I was a little concerned they were being 'too much' for this poor creature who'd been parachuted in to us, but Kelly said, 'It's fine, it's fine,' when I asked her. Laid-back and relaxed, nothing fazed her. Both she and her colleague were beaming as they watched the fun and games unfold.

After all the treats had been given and every child had taken sufficient turns at commanding him, the dog turned in a small half-circle and then lay down on the rug and went to sleep. He was so calm and chilled. And even though I knew he wasn't going to be our dog, even though I knew he would be going to another family, some small part of me still thought, *It feels like this dog belongs.*

Kelly, her colleague and the dog were with us for a good two hours. It was a magical afternoon. In the end, though, it was time for them to leave. Everybody gathered round and gave the doggy final cuddles and strokes and smiles.

And then we said goodbye to Sox.

As soon as he'd gone, I got the vacuum cleaner out and ran it over the cream carpet. ('Neil,' I said, 'we're going to need a better Hoover, this one's not picking up the hair!') But it wasn't just his hair that Sox left in the house. There was a palpable excitement, even after he'd gone. The whole house sort of buzzed for a bit; it was really nice.

That night, I tucked Toby into bed beneath his crunchy cotton duvet.

'Mummy …' he said to me.

'Yes, my darling?'

'Wouldn't it be *wonderful* if we could have a dog like Sox?'

I closed my eyes. *Yes, it would.*

'Mummy, what if it *was* Sox?'

I opened my eyes and looked down at him lying in his bed. He looked hopeful, so excited. He was a boy who had never enjoyed Christmas, but in that moment he looked exactly like a child who was dreaming of the best Christmas present he could possibly imagine.

'You know, Tobes, we don't know that it will be Sox – Sox has probably got an owner already. We just have to wait for the right one for us.'

At this he looked a bit crestfallen, so I quickly reassured him.

'Kelly is a very special lady and she will choose exactly the right dog for you, who is going to help you and be your best friend.'

'OK, Mummy,' he said sleepily. 'Night, night.'

'Night, night, Tobes. Sleep well.'

And he shut his eyes and dreamed … of a big black dog as tall as a house, with a heart as big as a castle.

17

Happy Ever After?

We tried to keep a lid on the kids' excitement. Honestly, we did.

'Kelly's visit with Sox was just the next stage in the process,' Neil or I would say, in a very sensible, sombre tone of voice. 'It could be a two-year wait before the dog for *our* family is available.'

'Oh yeah,' they'd say, 'yeah yeah ...' but you could see they really weren't listening to a word we said. For them, any minute now we could receive a phone call to say we were going to have a dog, and *that* was the important thing.

Dogs replaced dinosaurs as Toby's ultimate passion. I showed him the videos online of what the dogs could do and he loved that – not for their skills, but just for the fact of seeing the dogs. His eyes would light up and he'd go, 'Ooh!' He had an interest all of a sudden. It was lovely.

We told Toby that the dog, whoever he was, whenever he arrived, would be Toby's dog, really.

'He will be here to help you,' I said.

Toby was perplexed by that. 'Well, *how* is he going to help me?' he asked.

I told him about how the dogs could stop children from bolting, explaining, 'When you run, the dog runs after you and catches you.'

'Oh!' said Toby, in a very surprised voice.

'And if you keep running,' I said, 'he'll bite your leg off. And if you keep running again, he'll take your arm off. And then if you *still* keep on running, he'll just eat you.'

Toby was silent for a moment, considering. 'Mummy,' he said thoughtfully, 'was that a joke?'

'Yes, Tobes,' I replied seriously.

'Oh.' A little smile started twitching at the corners of his mouth. 'Oh!' A giggle rumbled up from his belly and popped out like a soda bubble. 'Oh – ho, ho, ho!' And he was off, laughing. Toby thought that was hilarious.

The entire family was energised by the idea of an assistance dog coming to help us. Despite my knowledge that we might have a two-year wait on our hands, I couldn't stop myself talking to all the kids about how different things would be *when the dog comes*. Conscious of everything Ollie had missed out on, the first thing I said to him was, 'It's going to be amazing – we can do this and do that and go there, and we can go out for lovely long walks with the dog and things like that, Ollie! We can go places and we can take the dog anywhere – which means *we* can go anywhere. Because we'll have the dog, and the dog will help Toby.'

Toby himself was super-excited. I think he thought, and certainly what I thought and what I probably fed into him, was that the dog was going to be like a magic wand and it would make everything better. Perhaps that was silly of me. I was putting all his hopes on one thing. But to be honest, all my hopes were pinned on it too.

Neil, as well, was buoyed up by the whole thing. He'd been particularly taken with Sox – well, all of us had. Toby still talked constantly about the big black dog who had visited our home when he and I had our chats in the car or just before bed. As for Neil, he confessed only to me that he thought Sox was *really* lovely – to the point where he even said, 'If they phone up and say you can have this dog but it's not Sox, well … I *really* want Sox,' he finished lamely.

About a week after Kelly's visit, we received an email from her to follow up, just giving us more information and asking if we'd made the changes to our house yet – the doggy loo area and the stairgate-guarded safe place. It had been a chaotic week, as usual, especially with the Easter holidays coming up, so we hadn't had a moment to think about it. We were surprised they'd come back to us so quickly about the changes given there wasn't a dog ready for us, but we took the hint.

'Neil,' I said urgently, 'get the toilet done!'

So Neil spent a weekend doing it. Kelly had just said 'email when you're done', so I quickly tapped out a message to her to say we were ready now and sent it off. But then we didn't hear anything more.

The Easter break of 2013 loomed: a holiday from the daily drive to Banbury and the chaos of term-time, but also two full weeks of the kids being cooped up at home. Lauren had revision timetables coming out of her ears and looked stressed and tense; Ollie was clearly bored, and I hadn't seen much of Joe or Toby as they spent most of their time in their rooms. With the positive buzz from Sox's visit still affecting everyone's mood, I thought, *I wonder ... I wonder if we might be able to manage a family day out.*

I broached it with Neil first. We'd got to the point by then where, even if we were all invited to a big important family do, we'd just be like, 'Oh God, how on earth are we going to *do* this?' and usually we wouldn't bother going as it was just too much tension and stress. There had been too many times where such occasions had ended badly so it was quite a big deal for us to decide to give it a go, but that was what we did. We both agreed that Toby seemed in quite a good frame of mind and the weather that Easter holiday was mild. Toby could be funny about going outside in certain kinds of weather, but we looked up the forecast for the final weekend of the holiday and it was a good temperature, it wasn't raining, it wasn't too windy, and so we thought we would *try*. I was desperate to get the kids out and about, for us all to have a day together as a family. Toby had been so much better lately – surely we would be OK?

We decided to go to the Natural History Museum in London. It offered something for everyone, and as we were going on a Sunday we could drive, which would be less disruption for Toby. We bundled all four kids into the car, Toby plugged into his headphones as usual, and headed off.

It was a bright spring day and I felt *normal* as we travelled into the capital. *There must be lots of other families spending this day together*, I thought, *just like us.* All the kids were happy and looking forward to their day at the museum. They were all quite science-mad, and of course Toby had his love of dinosaurs, so it seemed a really good choice for a day they could all enjoy.

We arrived and joined the long snaking queue leading up to the front door. Toby stayed plugged into his earphones. Nevertheless, you could see him start to get agitated. He began rocking back and forth. We inched forward in the queue and I just thought, *Come on, come on, we're nearly there …*

'How long is it going to be?' Toby demanded. He was wringing his hands anxiously.

'Not long now …' I said, crossing my fingers.

We inched forward again. 'Mummy …' Toby began.

And then there was the usual litany of complaints and demands, all the way inside. By the time we arrived in the entrance hall with its stupendous dinosaur skeleton, Toby had been fed and watered dozens of times – but we were all in. We had made it. There was a further delay as every child wanted to visit the facilities, and I could see all the waiting and the faffing getting to Toby, who crossed and uncrossed his arms and huffed and puffed, but he kept himself together and we all headed up to the rock exhibition on the top floor of the museum.

It's obvious how you're supposed to visit a museum. All the display boards are laid out in a nice linear manner and it was apparent to Toby that you read them all in order and every single word. As he proceeded to do everything by the book, he tutted as people pushed in; he took a deep breath as someone blocked his view. It was very busy, and very pushy and shovy, and I could see him trying to control himself.

He got to a display board about the Aberfan disaster, in which 116 children and 28 adults were killed by the catastrophic collapse of a colliery spoil tip in 1966. While he was sensibly reading the words, trying to take it all in, all around him his elbows were being knocked and there was shouting and chatting and people pushing past him. As I watched him, it was like seeing him disintegrate. He couldn't keep the steam in anymore and the tears came, hot and fast and cross on his cheeks. All the tension of the day – the journey and the going outside, the queue, the waiting for his siblings, the crowds, the display – it all just got too much.

The other kids were still poring over the exhibition, exclaiming over their discoveries and pointing out bits and pieces to Neil. I intercepted Toby.

'Mummy, I don't want to see anymore. I can't do it anymore!' he cried. Everything had added and added and added to the point where it was too much for him. 'I don't want to go anywhere else, it's too noisy.'

'We'll go for lunch, then, Toby,' I said, trying to distract him.

I gathered the others and we plodded all the way down the stairs to the bottom of the building, where there's a dining area in the basement, where you can eat your packed lunch. Toby was in floods of tears. I left Neil to sort out the others and I took Toby off into a little corner, just the two of us. It was next to a fire exit or a bin or something; there was no one else around. He sat down on the floor and turned away from me, letting the tears stream down his cheeks.

I sat down on the floor next to him.

'Want a hug, Tobes?'

'No,' he muttered. And then the horribly familiar refrain: 'I don't deserve a hug, Mummy. You'd be better off without me. You'd be better off if I'd never ever been born.'

I stroked his back from behind.

'That's not true, Toby Turner,' I said. 'I love you.'

I kept on stroking him, and he kept on crying, and in the end he let me hold him tight and rock him. Eventually, he twisted round in my arms and gave me a proper cuddle as I whispered soothing words to him, and we both curled up on the floor and *hugged* as hard as we could.

We were there for about an hour as the other children sat with Neil and ate their lunch. I don't know if any passers-by saw me and Tobes sitting there embracing on the floor; over time you become hardened to strangers' looks and sighs anyway. I didn't care what anyone else might think as I was fully focused on Toby. I tried to bring him back to me so I said in a calm but jolly manner, 'Shall we go and have a look at what else we can find? What about that big dinosaur in the lobby? Wasn't he something, eh?'

He agreed to come with me and the whole family traipsed slowly along to where the big skeleton was suspended above us. But I could see that Toby wasn't settling; he wasn't interested and engaged anymore, he was just in this anxious state. We'd found before that you could keep the lid on it for a little bit, but it's like putting a lid on a saucepan full to the brim with boiling water; eventually, catastrophe will ensue. Toby had broken, and he couldn't put himself back together again.

Neil and I exchanged a glance. We both knew it was game over.

'You know what?' I said to everyone. 'I think we'll go home.'

It was only just after lunch, but we all walked out of the museum and back to the car. I could tell the other children would have absolutely liked to stay longer – after all, we had only visited one room in the entire museum, plus the dinosaur lobby – but they didn't say a word. There was a kind of resignation about their downward-sloping shoulders and their soft, disappointed sighs. By now, Toby's meltdowns were just a normal, to-be-expected part of their lives.

Neil swung the car out of the car park and started the long drive home.

'We'll come back again,' I said brightly to the children in the back. 'Daddy picked up a leaflet, so we'll plan what we're going to see and we can come any Sunday we like in the future!'

No one said anything in return. I turned back to face the front and stared out of the windscreen. *I felt this was such a good idea this morning*, I thought to myself, *but it really* wasn't *a good idea.*

Toby just couldn't manage, that was the long and short of it. He couldn't manage a family day out. He couldn't manage a formal school environment. He could barely manage a single minute of his day without me there.

I thought of what I always told the children. *When the dog comes …*

But none of us knew when that might be. And would the magic wand *really* work? Wasn't that just for fairy stories?

I closed my eyes and wished and wished and *wished* for a happy ever after.

18

A Dog Called Sox

Ring, ring … Ring, ring …

The phone sounded in the house one Thursday afternoon. It was a rare moment of being alone; Toby was with Lorna, his ILT (he had just started to trust her enough to take a lesson on his own, if it was a good day), and the other kids were at school. It was partway through April 2013, just a week or so after our disastrous trip to London.

For some strange reason, I started as I heard the phone begin to burr and almost gasped a little to myself. *Better get it* – the thought went through my mind, before I could stop it – *it could be a dog.*

I don't know why I thought that, but as I picked up the phone I could feel my heart hammering in my chest.

'Vikky?' said the voice on the other end. 'It's Kelly. What are you doing the week of 13 May?'

'Why?' I said slowly, not wanting to get too excited. Perhaps it was just another interview, yet another questionnaire.

'Would you like Sox?'

Would we … *What?* With hindsight, it's obvious that they had paired us with Sox from the start and had simply needed to ensure the match was perfect before giving us the green light – but this was the very first we knew of it. So … *squeal!* There was *lots* of squealing. It was just … I don't know what I said, what I felt, I just remember *squealing!* We were getting a dog! And not just any dog – we were getting super Sox!

I was gabbling on the phone to Kelly. 'I'll have to talk to Neil about the dates,' I managed, 'but yes, yes, yes, yes, *yes!*'

I heard her laughing at my reaction. 'Look,' she said – and there was a smile in her voice – 'you need to calm down. Just calm down a little bit. You need to ring me to confirm tomorrow, but you've got twenty-four hours. I'll give you twenty-four hours to think about it.'

Think about it! I'd been thinking of nothing else ever since I'd first gone on their website! But Kelly insisted – some people, she said, do need to think about it and talk about it with their families.

'Ring me up in the morning,' she said as she signed off, 'and let me know for sure.'

After replacing the handset, I immediately dialled Neil at work. I blabbered out the news to him as quickly as I could, barely pausing for breath.

'Oh my God!' said Neil. 'Oh, wow, that's amazing!'

The excitement between us was like nothing you've ever known.

'Can you do that?' I said to him. 'Can you cover those dates?' Kelly had explained that the reason she'd asked about the week of the thirteenth was because I would need to come away for a whole week's residential training with our dog – with Sox! – so it was a lot to ask of Neil as he'd be responsible for all four kids while I was away.

'Yep, yep, we'll do it,' he said, almost yelling in his exhilaration, 'we'll sort it out.'

After we'd hung up, I didn't know what to do with myself. I pulled my mobile from my pocket and typed out a text message.

We've got Sox!

I found two numbers in my contacts – Lauren Mobile, Joe Mobile – and pressed *send*.

A reply came back straight away from my daughter.

What do you mean 'We've got Sox'?

Sox the dog! I typed back feverishly, barely able to believe it.

There was real excitement and Lauren and Joe and I had texts flying back and forth. Lorna was going to drop Toby back for me and so the older two were home before him. We were all so thrilled. None of us could wait to tell Toby. There was such a buzz in the house, it was palpable. It was like I'd said Christmas was going to be tomorrow or something. Everyone had happy faces and shining eyes.

We heard the car outside and then we heard Toby's heavy footsteps coming up to the front door.

'We've got to tell him, Mum, we've *got* to tell him!' cried Lauren and Joe. 'You tell him, as soon as he comes through the door!'

And so as soon as Toby came into the hallway, I went up to him and I took his hands, which I sometimes do. It helps to calm him. As I tried to look him right in the eye, I could see him thinking, *What is it ...?* Lauren and Joe were hanging about behind me, delight rolling off them in waves of joy.

'Do you remember Sox, Toby? The dog who came to visit us?' I asked him. (I knew he did, because he'd often talked about him, but it didn't hurt to ask.)

He nodded, slowly, as though he didn't quite trust himself. I think he was wondering what was up.

'Did you *really* like him?' I went on.

He nodded again, his green eyes looking hesitantly, hopefully into mine.

'Well,' I said. I couldn't help grinning then. 'Kelly's just rung me ... and she said *we're* going to have him.'

Toby gasped. '*Really?*'

'Yes,' I said. '*Really.*'

He made a surprised noise. 'Oh!' And then, to *my* surprise, he did a bit of a jig and he gave me a big warm hug and he said, 'Oh, that's *so* exciting!'

It was just ... *lovely*. There is no other word for it. Toby was jigging and Lauren and Joe and I were laughing and there was such joy, such unadulterated joy, in our wooden-floored hallway.

'That's *really* good!' cried Toby.

I could see his mind going *tick, tick, tick, tick*.

'When?' he asked next. 'When will Sox be here?'

'In about three or four weeks,' I said.

I could see his shoulders dip a bit; see him thinking, *Oh, so it's not now. I've got to wait.*

'Toby,' I said, 'it's actually a good thing Sox isn't coming right away, because we have an awful lot to do to get ready for his arrival. Would you like to help me get his things set up?'

'Oh, yes, *please*, Mummy!' he said with great excitement.

And it wasn't just Toby who wanted to help – oh no, this was a full-blown, full-on Turner family affair. I kept them all involved, every single child – and Neil as well. 'Let's get on the Internet and choose a really nice bed!' I said. And so we all pored over the webpages and pointed out our favourites and in the end we picked out a top-of-the-range memory-foam dog bed, with a luxurious fleece cover ... because he was worth it!

'Now,' I said to everyone, 'where do you think his bed should go?'

And that involved a lot of family decision-making and planning as well. Sox's bed and bowls were set up for ages before he was due to come home and it was really nice seeing them sitting there, knowing what was coming; how different things would be.

To be honest, though, even before Sox got there, such was his amazing power that the very *idea* of him seemed to have an effect on Toby. Sox was obviously the main topic of conversation at all times and everyone had a different suggestion of what we had to get for him before he came to live with us. With all that we needed to buy, we decided that we'd have to make a special family shopping trip to go and pick it all up. I chose a quiet time for this and we all piled into the car and from there into the pet store. Every child picked out a special something to give to Sox from them as an individual. One chose a tennis ball, another a pulley toy, and so on. Toby selected a soft toy, a long squeaky monkey – just from him to his new best friend.

Throughout the trip, Toby behaved impeccably.

And he didn't wear his headphones.

I think he was so excited about Sox that he left the house without even thinking about it. I don't think there was any thought process there at all. He simply walked outside, hopped into the car, went shopping for his dog and came home again – like any ordinary boy would do.

It was lovely.

Toby was full of chatter about Sox in the intervening weeks before my training. He talked about him a lot. He kept planning things: 'When we get Sox, we can do this. And when it's nice weather, with Sox here we can do that.'

I, too, was trying to open him up to all the things we could do once Sox had arrived.

'We can go for long walks, Tobes,' I said. Neil and I both missed being able to take long walks with the family. 'Perhaps we could even go to the forest …'

Toby simply nodded – there was no mention of a tent or even a water-purifying system, which was what he usually piped up about when we mentioned a family trip to the Great Outdoors.

'We could go back to the forest and take the dog for a walk,' I added happily. 'Just think of all those wonderful things we can do!'

There was just one family member missing from all the excitement now … and he was *our* dog called Sox.

19

Back to School

Monday, 13 May 2013 – the first day of the rest of my life. It felt very, very strange being on my own as I drove to the residential training course. I had never left the children before so I actually found that really hard, but the moment I walked into the training centre (which was in Banbury, of all places!) there was just a really lovely atmosphere and so I relaxed and enjoyed myself. Though not too much – I was, after all, there to work.

The training courses are very intimate. It would just be me and two other mums, all of us learning how to train our dogs together. Or rather, I should say, *we* were the ones being trained; the dogs already knew it all – we were the clueless amateurs who had to pick it up!

I was assigned a room and headed there to unpack. On the door was a sign: *Vikky and Sox*. That was a lovely touch. The room was very nice, with a bathroom and twin beds and a tiny little telly up on top of the wardrobe. The training centre is often used for physically disabled people so it had a kind of hospital feel to it – the beds were electric – but they'd made it cosy and it had patio doors that opened onto a terrace, which was very pretty. So this was my home for the next five nights ...

Once I'd unpacked, I headed back to the communal area and was immediately given all the equipment Sox and I would need for our busy week ahead: blue assistance-dog jacket for Sox, harnesses, leads and clips ...

It was here I met my 'classmates' for the first time too. First, I was introduced to Lindsey, who was a really nice woman with long blonde curly hair. She had a little girl with autism who was only three years old, but despite her daughter's young age Lindsey was already incredibly switched on about all the support organisations and the things you could get for autistic kids. I think she knew even more than me! She was a mine of information.

Claire, bless her, was late because her child's school had assumed he was coming with her and she'd had to sort out all of that before she could join us. I could just imagine the stress. When she arrived, she made her apologies and we all welcomed her. She wore her hair in a practical blonde bob, not dissimilar to mine. As we got chatting, I discovered her son was only a year younger than Toby.

As all three of us began sharing stories around the table in the communal area, I learned that both Claire and Lindsey's children had much higher needs than Toby. Straight away, we all hit it off. I think sometimes when you've got something in common with people you do, don't you? I'd never had any interaction with other parents of autistic children before – I'd never had any time even to go on the Internet forums or anything – and actually I found it was really nice. They were both lovely ladies and we all felt an immediate bond.

'Right then,' said Kelly, who was leading the course. 'Let's get started. If I could ask you all please to go to your rooms and wait there, I will bring your dogs to you one by one.'

With a thrill of anticipation and some trepidation, we all headed back to the residential corridor and entered our private rooms. As I sat down on my bed I could hear Kelly bringing a dog up the corridor. She knocked on Lindsey's door and I heard Lindsey greeting her dog, who was called Gunner. Then I heard Kelly leaving again and I thought, *It's me next ...*

Click-clack, click-clack ... A dog's claws sounded on the floor. *Here he comes ...*

My door opened and suddenly Sox was there. He was *very* excited! (He wasn't the only one.) He was too well trained to jump up, but he came rushing into the room on his long legs and gave me a good hard sniff as I tousled his inky black ears. He was even taller than I remembered.

'Hello, Sox, *hello*!' I said to him.

'He's very excited today!' Kelly commented, watching us greet each other.

I'd love to say it was because he remembered me, but to be honest I think he'd encountered so many people in his short doggy life that he now just accepted them, whoever they were. Yet that friendly acceptance is really all a part of his very special charm.

'Right,' said Kelly, back to business, 'I'm going to go and get Bessie for Claire now. I'm going to leave you here in the room for a bit with your dog, and then we're all going to go down to the training hall together.'

With that, she gently shut the door behind her. Sox and I were left alone.

I sat down on the floor next to him. Almost following my lead, he lay down and stretched himself out along the whole length of my leg. I could feel his warmth and his weight right next to me: a solid, dependable dog. I stroked him constantly, running my hands all over his soft fur, and he bent his head into my palm to get even more pressure, to feel even closer to me. I couldn't stop thinking, *He's ours, he's ours, I can't believe it, he's ours …* It felt magical. From the very first minute we were alone, it was magical.

'It's you and me now, Sox,' I said to him. He looked at me solemnly with his bottomless brown eyes, which seemed full of understanding and smart good sense. There was a genuine feeling of collaboration – that we were going to be working as a team to help Toby, and together we were going to make things better. Sox was the answer – the puzzle piece we'd been missing. As I sat and stroked him I couldn't stop thinking: *This is our future.* And then: *It's going to be* amazing …

I felt incredibly emotional. After everything we'd been through, and all the waiting for this very special dog, it was a moment of: *Wow, we're here! This is it.*

It was a moment worth waiting for.

After ten minutes or so, Kelly returned for stage one of our training. I picked up Sox's lead, which was a leather cord with a high-vis flash on it saying 'Dogs for the Disabled'. We'd just be working with the lead today; the jacket work and the harness training would come later in the week. I got the lead clipped onto his collar without too much ado, and then we faced our first challenge: getting out of the room.

The training started straight away. And the training said: Sox must sit before I open a door. As we approached it, he had to sit, and then I had to open the door while he was still sitting, and then I had to walk through first, with Sox following in my footsteps. Sounds simple, right? It wasn't! The process was something I'd never encountered before. Good old Dusty, Neil's Golden Retriever, used to go through doors behind you, in front, and sometimes twisting round your legs and almost tripping you up. But that hadn't mattered because he wasn't a working dog. I learned right away that everything about Sox was different. Everything had to be a certain way because, when he was working, he was on a mission, and as his handler I had to make sure we both played by the rules.

So even getting through the door was a meal in itself, but eventually Sox and I mastered it together and we made it out into the corridor. Lesson one was done; lesson two was how to walk. He had to be on the left-hand side of me and he had to have his shoulder a specific distance away from my leg so that he wasn't pulling ahead of me and was ready for his next command.

The route to the training hall took us via several doors and down a couple of flights of stairs. Each time we encountered such an 'obstacle', we had to stop and go through the same drill. 'Sox, sit,' I would say. He would plonk his bottom on the floor and I would reach for the door, pull it wide and walk through, at which point he'd follow. If Sox got too eager and lifted his haunches while the door was being opened, I had to close it and start again from the top. When we reached stairs, we'd have to stop and wait until I had commanded Sox to move; he could only walk upon my word. It felt like it took over an hour just to get to the training hall, but every single minute we were learning. It was quite mind-boggling, actually, but bit by bit, we were getting better.

In the hall, we started with the basics, just walking round and getting a feel for it. After lunch, Kelly took us all outside to a quiet street and we did the same thing, but outside the road kerbs were our doors and flights of stairs, and each time we reached a road Sox had to sit and wait for my command before we crossed.

Even that was hard – much harder than I'd anticipated. I had to say, 'Sox, to the kerb,' to let him know what was up, but I had to make sure I did it so many paces back from the kerb and simultaneously slow my pacing down and control Sox on the lead too. It was a bit like patting your head and rubbing your tummy in a circle, but with a big dog on a lead and a range of commands and actions to get your head around. Bearing in mind we would eventually have to add a small autistic child to this equation, I could see why the training was going to last a week!

I think we all did pretty well on the first day. As I say, the dogs really knew it all already, so us mums were the ones playing catch-up. For the dogs, what they had to learn was our body language and the differing tones of our voices, and that must surely have been child's play in comparison. It really was rather challenging! Occasionally, I could see Sox looking up at me with a comical roll of his eyes as though to say, 'Oh God, she's not very good at this, is she?' as I fumbled some easy command or another. He'd give an indulgent sigh and then carry on with what he was supposed to do, but as the day went on he gave me fewer and fewer quizzical looks, and our bond grew closer the more I learned. Sometimes he would be a little slow at command and Kelly rationalised to me, 'He's a big dog, it just takes a while for the message to get there!'

It was a really intense day, with Claire and Bessie, Lindsey and Gunner, and Sox and me all working extremely hard. By the end of it, I think each mum-and-dog duo felt a real sense of camaraderie – which was just as it should be, and just as Kelly had intended. The dogs would be with us 24/7 now (except when we ate, during which time they rested in our rooms). It was really important that the dogs bonded with us mums throughout the course, because at the end of the week we'd be taking them out of this familiar environment and putting them into our homes, and the only person they would know there would be us. So it was essential that each of us formed a strong relationship with our hound.

The other dogs were also clever little things (though of course I believed they were not a patch on Sox!). Gunner was a tiny black Labrador – toy-sized compared to Sox – who was extremely perky. When he walked, he trotted like a horse, and he kept on looking up at Lindsey as if to say keenly, 'What am I going to do now? What am I going to do? Tell me, tell me, tell me!' He was shiny-coated and had very handsome features.

Bessie was the boss of both the boys. She was about three years old so she was older than the others, and in fact she'd already been with a family before where the match hadn't worked out, so she knew the business and was very much in charge. A small barrel of energy, she was another black Lab, and she had this command about her, almost as though the other dogs were a little in awe of her; it was really weird.

For all us mums, it was the first time we'd ever been away from our families. You might have thought that would make us lonely and keen to socialise in the evening, but as much as we all got on really well, once dinner was over, each of us retreated to our rooms to spend time with our dogs. I think we all just wanted to be with them.

That first evening, I walked into our room after dinner and shut the door behind me. Sox had got up to greet me; now, he turned in a small half-circle and lay down comfortably on the floor, and I sat with him so we could have a little cuddle. Already, he was feeling like a friend – and I think the feeling was mutual. That first night together, we got no sleep at all for every time I rolled over in bed, he would get up out of his and come over to me.

'Hmmm?' he seemed to say as he came to investigate. 'What is it? Is there something I can do to help?'

It was just constant, throughout the night. Every bed squeak elicited a keen 'Hello!' from Sox. I tried to ignore him, but eventually I thought with an indulgent smile, *Oh, I can't* ... At about 4 a.m. I gave up the ghost and got out of bed so we could have a cuddle on the floor. An hour later, the sun came up. A new day of training was beginning.

There was so much to learn. As the course unfolded, we graduated to harness walking. The harness is used when Sox goes into a public place, like a shopping centre. And with the harness, everything changes again: Sox has to walk on the right side of me as opposed to the left and I have to command him to do more complex manoeuvres. Inevitably, the harness work took us straight back into the training room before we could be trusted on the streets. Eventually, though, we progressed from the training room to quiet streets, and from there to busy roads – with both the leads and the harness – and then finally we made it to the pinnacle of our training: a visit to a thriving shopping centre, where we went round all the shops with the dogs and really got a sense of how they could transform our lives. Because they are assistance dogs, you can take them anywhere, just as you can with guide dogs. I could see at once that Sox was metaphorically going to open so many doors for us as a family. (Of course, it had to be only metaphorically – in reality, he would have to sit still and *I* would open the door …)

Each night, I emailed photos home of what we'd been up to and spoke to the kids on the phone. I was missing them like mad. They, of course, had only one thing on their minds.

'Hello!' I would say to Toby. 'You'll never guess what I learned today!'

But Toby wasn't interested. 'How's Sox?' was always the first thing he wanted to know.

I would tell him all about what we'd been doing through the day and then he'd go off and do something else. It was never: 'I miss you, Mummy', it was always: 'How's Sox?'

Sox, I was delighted to see, was in fact very, very well. He'd settled down after the second night and the two of us were now as close as peas in a pod. You could see him listening to me more and more and Kelly even said to me at one point, 'You know what? He's really bonded with you much quicker than I thought he would.' Coming from the professional, that was high praise indeed.

Certainly he was always keen to see me. He welcomed me so enthusiastically if I'd been away from our room, even for just a few minutes. He's not allowed to jump up on people but he would leap to his feet as soon as he heard the door open, and when he saw it was me, he would make this pleased huffy sound that he has and then wag his tail so hard that his whole body was going. It was a truly lovely greeting.

On the Wednesday night, we had a real breakthrough. As usual, Lindsey and Claire and I had made our excuses and retreated to our rooms to spend the evening with our dogs. As Sox and I sat cuddling on the floor, he leaned his weight into me, rolled over and showed me his belly. You know dogs are really comfortable with you when they do that.

'Oh, Sox!' I said happily, as I rubbed his tummy and he huffed with pleasure. He really was our dog now.

Come the Thursday night, I arranged a little treat for myself and Sox. I'd been missing my family so much, and Banbury, I persuaded myself, really wasn't *that* far away from Bicester after all, so I asked Kelly if it would be OK if they came to visit. She said yes, so Neil and I agreed that he would bring all the kids straight after school to visit Sox and me at the training centre.

I waited in the car park for them, I was that excited. I'd left Sox in the room so we didn't overwhelm him, so I stood on my own in the warm spring air, simply waiting for them to arrive. I was so eager to see them all.

I remember the car pulling up like it was yesterday. My heart was racing. I'd never been away from the children before and our reunion was just lovely – I got enormous hugs from them all. Hugs all round. Neil wrapped me in his arms and gave me a squeeze and a kiss and I beamed at him.

'Come on, everyone,' I said happily, 'let's go into the lounge area. I'll go and get Sox. Toby, would you like to come with me?'

He nodded shyly, and together we walked to my room. It was so gorgeous to be reunited with him. I really hoped he and Sox would get on well. This was crunch time. For the first time, Toby would be meeting his dog, knowing Sox *was* his dog.

'Here we go then, Tobes. This is us.'

We paused outside the door. I could see Toby was a bit hesitant, and as we opened the door and Sox went into his excited 'Hello! I haven't seen you for five minutes but it feels like it's been five *millennia*!' routine, he looked even more unsure. Sox was wagging his tail like he was about to take off and Toby paused on the threshold.

'It's OK,' I said. 'He's just a bit excited about seeing you. He'll calm down in a minute.'

We walked into the room and Sox backed up a little bit.

'Sit, Sox,' I said calmly.

At once, his bottom went down and he sat tall and proud and still on the floor. He was looking at Toby, his head angled on one side, his eyes clear and understanding. But he stayed very still, just as he'd been trained, and Toby visibly relaxed and felt more comfortable. My son walked confidently into the room.

'Hello, Sox, how are you?' he said. He came right up to Sox and gave him a big fuss. 'You've had a busy week, haven't you? Are you looking after my mummy? I hope you are. I've heard all about your adventures! What a busy boy you've been …'

My word ... I thought. He was *chattering*. Toby Turner was chattering. With other children, with every other child he'd ever encountered, he had always been awkward about introducing himself or holding a conversation. As a rule, he's just not very good at chit-chat. But this was completely different. You couldn't shut him up!

Meanwhile, Sox was looking at Toby. There was almost this bubble around the pair of them; I couldn't quite put my finger on it. There was just this different feeling, a different feeling that had been magicked up now they were together at last. A relaxed calmness had come over them both, and they were together in this bubble.

But then, I realised, it wasn't like a bubble; it wasn't a wall that had come up and shielded them, cutting Toby off from the world like his audiobooks did. In contrast, he and Sox were both in this room with me, sharing this special moment, and the waves of calm from them both included me, too. Toby was smiling and chattering and he was calm and relaxed.

It's going to work, I thought. I felt like crying, but it was too happy a moment for tears, even tears of joy. *It really IS going to work. It's going to be lovely.*

'Hey, Tobes,' I said, almost not wanting to break the spell, but conscious of the other children waiting, 'shall we take him into the lounge now?'

'Yes, Mummy,' said Toby, and together he and Sox and I walked back into the lounge. The calm feeling came with us. And it seemed to blossom out over the entire family. No one shouted or pushed in or fought over the dog; everyone was just happy to be in his presence.

As for Sox, he was quite extraordinary. He went and sat with Neil for a bit of fuss. My husband reached down to him with his large hands and gave him a nice scratch behind the ears and a smooth rub-down on his furry black coat. Neil has always been a dog man, and it was brilliant to see him with a dog again – almost like old times. I caught his eye and smiled.

And then Sox got up and went to the next person. Taking it in turns, he went round every member of our family and said a very special hello. There was Joe, so quiet and reserved, happily playing with Sox. Lauren, who was midway through her GCSEs, seemed to let out a little sigh of relief as she gave Sox a big cuddle. Ollie, meanwhile, appeared fairly docile as he petted Sox, but I couldn't rule out the possibility that he was already planning a world-dominating *Britain's Got Talent* routine featuring Sox for his TV debut … Who knew?

And all the while Toby sat calm and content, occasionally ruffling Sox's fur, but completely at ease as the other children said their hellos and started to form their own friendships with his dog.

There was a strange familiarity about the situation that I couldn't quite identify. As I sat close to Neil, watching our family play with the dog, I realised what it was. It felt like we were introducing another child to our brood. It was as if we were introducing a child who was going to be with us forever, it was that sort of feeling – and it was really, really lovely.

Sox, by this point, was lying upside down on the floor with his legs in the air. All the children were gathered round him, tickling his belly. He looked like the dog who'd got the cream, the cat and the butcher's sausages.

And I knew exactly how he felt.

After that, it wasn't too hard waving goodbye to my family. I knew I only had two nights left, and actually I was very much enjoying the full night's sleep I was getting at the centre. I'd forgotten how rejuvenating proper sleep could be.

But most rejuvenating of all was the feeling I'd got from seeing Sox with Toby.

It's going to be all right, I thought to myself, as Sox and I turned in for the night in our cosy little room. *Everything's going to be just fine.*

20

Home at Last

On the Friday afternoon, as a treat for all our hard work – that of Claire, Lindsey and me, but also Bessie, Gunner and Sox – we took the dogs for a free run. That was so lovely. All the dogs had been working so hard the whole week and they hadn't really had any free doggy time where they could just be dogs, because they were always either training or bonding with us mums. Kelly stressed that it was really important, especially once we were home, that the dogs had time off where they could just be dogs – no harness, no lead, no work: just the wind in their fur and a world of scents and smells to explore.

The weather was absolutely atrocious. I'm not kidding. Mud up to your knees! We'd taken them all in one car and that was funny in itself; little Bessie sat regally in the boot, heaps of space around her, while Gunner and Sox squashed themselves into the corner and barely dared to look at her, as though by royal decree.

Once they were running free, however, all bets were off. It was so great to see them just being normal dogs. And it was complete mud madness – they were charging around and woofing their heads off and clearly having the most enormous amount of fun.

It gave me a bit of an insight into Sox's personality, actually, because at work he can be very contained and focused. Now, off duty, he was, well, a little bit bonkers! He was surprisingly bolshie. To see him in the training room you'd think he had quite a submissive personality, but now he really showed off his assertive streak and revealed to me that actually he was quite a strong dog.

All week long Bessie and Gunner, who were both older than him, had been in charge. But now Sox was giving them a run for their money, playfully shoulder-barging them and instigating some play-fighting as they tussled and rolled and ran in the mud. For all his posturing, though, Sox couldn't quite conceal his youth. He was pretty clumsy on his legs, as though he hadn't quite grown into them yet; he reminded me of Bambi.

After a while, we called time on the fun and practised recalls with the dogs. Unlike Toby, who always used to go AWOL when playtime was over, Sox was a star pupil at returning when called and lining up for home time. We piled all three dogs into the car and then headed back to the centre. Once there, baths were a necessity – for us all! The dogs were so filthy that everyone had got covered in mud. But it was actually really nice to give Sox a hose down and get him all clean again – ready for his homecoming the very next day.

I can still remember driving down the motorway with Sox sitting in the back of my car for the very first time. It was so exciting! I was also a little nervous, feeling the responsibility for him: *He's ours now, we've got to make sure everything's all right for him.* Part of the training had been looking out for our dogs getting stressed, so I knew if Sox started scratching, yawning or getting a bit panty it was a warning sign and I should take him away to chill out, but he seemed really relaxed right now.

When we arrived, the first thing I did was to walk him through the house and show him where his toilet area was out in the garden, because that's what Kelly had told us to do. Amazingly, the dogs only go to the toilet on command (I wish you could do that with children!). We had to say, 'Busy busy,' and then he'd perform. So he had a sniff around there and did his business and then he came back into the kitchen and sat down. The hardest thing was trying to keep the children calm. 'He's here for a long time now, you can just let him chill,' I kept saying, as they all crowded round his bed and just *stared*.

On his first day, Sox had a little shadow, and his name was Toby Turner. Toby was following him around all the time. Sox had free run of the house so we just let him wander as and where he wanted to, and every time he decided to explore a new room, Toby would also get up and pad after him to see what he was up to.

'Is he OK in there?' he would ask me.

'Yeah, he's fine, Toby. See how happy he is?'

And Sox would wag his tail, almost on cue.

Toby just always wanted to be with Sox. It was lovely. He wanted to see where Sox was and what he was doing, and he was always checking he was all right. Normally, Toby spent most of his time upstairs, playing in his bedroom on his own, but immediately he was downstairs much more often, which meant he felt more part of the family.

The connection between him and Sox was immediate. It was an instant friendship. That Saturday night, as I tucked my son into bed for the first time in a week, I said to him, 'So, Tobes, how does it feel with Sox here at last?'

He gave a contented little sigh. 'I just love him so much, Mummy,' he said. 'It's like having a special friend.'

And these friends had work to do together. Even once we were home, our training continued. Kelly came out every other day to keep drilling us. We were doing the same sort of things as on the course, but in the home environment and on the surrounding streets, and then came the time to attach Toby and Sox with the harness.

I sold the slow training process to Toby as him learning to look after his dog and something that the two of us were doing together, Mummy and Toby, but to be honest I don't think he needed any encouragement. He took it on as a responsibility and did a great job; he was really, really brilliant. It was a big confidence booster for him, actually. He walked a little bit taller.

In time, Toby learned all about the harness and the clips, and it became his job to sort it all out whenever we were going anywhere. He has his own clip, which is a bit like a belt that slots together, and then that clips onto a lead that attaches to Sox's harness, and then on the other side there's the lead connected to the dog's collar, which I use. Sox walks on my right-hand side when he's in harness, and Toby is then to the right of Sox. We go all in a line, a dynamic trio, taking the world by storm.

And that's exactly what we did.

From the very beginning, instantly, Toby no longer needed his cap or his hood, his headphones or his audiobooks when we went out. There was a different focus, because we were centred on the dog and what we were doing; we weren't focusing on Toby and how he was going to deal with things. The whole mood had lifted. And as the weather cleared and hot sunny days began to be the norm, Neil and I held our breath because normally Toby would never go out when it was hot; and those sunny days in the late May of 2013 were getting really hot and sweaty. But he was fine with it. He still got very warm, because he was a hot bod, but it didn't *bother* him in the slightest – because of Sox being there.

The biggest change, though, was his talking. As Kelly, Sox, Toby and I headed out for our training sessions, Toby never shut up. Seriously – he never, *ever* shut up! That spring he was into Greek gods, and poor Kelly constantly had to listen to monologue after monologue on Greek divinity as I concentrated on where we were going and what instructions I had to give the dog. Kelly always stood behind us, offering the odd bit of direction to me and giving suggestions from the back, and, meanwhile, Toby would be firing off all these facts at her as he walked beside Sox. She was brilliant with him, I have to say. In his little professor way, he would challenge her to find out some facts of her own, and I would secretly email her the answers so she could come back with them the next day and stun him with her knowledge. He was properly interacting: give and take, ebb and flow, talk and listen and share. I couldn't believe the transformation.

About a week after Sox had come home, Kelly was putting us through our paces once more. You have to pass an examination to become a fully qualified dog handler and so she was preparing me ready for the test, which would be in another week's time. As at the training centre, Kelly had been incrementally increasing our challenges, and now she started practising the test route we would eventually take with the examiner. This would involve heading out from home, going round the block – and then further afield: into town, through the shopping centre … really challenging stuff.

We were all hooked up together in the harness, with Kelly walking a little way behind as usual. I felt so apprehensive. At the end of the day, anything could happen. Was Toby really prepared for a shop? What if he bolted? What if he got upset?

We walked down the main street. We walked successfully through a shop: no meltdowns. We crossed a busy road – and another; and another. I was aware of Toby, who was sauntering along happily in the sunshine, not a care in the world, but primarily I was focused on what I was doing with the dog and which way we were going. Kelly prompted me with directions and I followed her as obediently as Sox did my commands.

I was so focused on the dog that, in the end, the final destination of our excursion took me by surprise. We all sat down in a coffee shop and had a drink. We would never, *ever* have done that with Toby before. But my son had a drink and embarked on yet another lecture on the fascinating topic of the Greek gods and he was happy. Nothing around him bothered him: not the noise of the coffee machines or the hum of people's chatter; not the people themselves, squeezing past our table or queuing by the door. Not a single thing was out of joint.

It was really weird.

Gosh, I thought, *we're sat here in a coffee shop. We haven't done this before.* It was a very surreal moment.

And we're sat here like everybody else, I thought, a little stunned. *The only thing different is that we have a dog under the table.*

But the coffee shop was only the start of it. I'm proud to say we passed the qualification walk first time. Now, we knew we could take Sox anywhere. Somewhat prosaically, I think our first trip out independently was the school run.

Previously, when I'd dropped Ollie off at school Toby would come with us, and he'd have to have his headphones and everything on and he wouldn't talk to anybody. Not a soul. In fact, he'd be so bubbled up in his own world that I would basically steer him to Ollie's classroom door, sit him on a chair at the side, drop Ollie in and then pick up Toby, steer him back through the corridors and then back to the car – and that's what we did, every school day of the week. Even though it was only a fifteen-minute walk from our house to the school, we always drove – because Toby couldn't cope with the chaos of 'outside'.

With Sox as our escort, however, we decided now that we *would* walk to school. I can remember with crystal clarity the first time we did it, three weeks after Sox had come home. Toby got the harness sorted and attached himself to the dog as his friend stood solidly by his side, sturdy as a big black doggy mountain. I had Sox's lead in one hand and little Ollie's in the other.

Toby chatted to his brother and Sox and me all the way there. Not only that – as we turned for home, we heard a voice behind us.

'Yoo-hoo! Vikky, Toby!' we heard. There was only one loud cheery voice like that I knew from the school playground.

'*Katie!*' I said with pleasure, as she came up to us. She'd been seeing her kids off to school as well and she'd spotted us and the new doggy addition to our family as we'd waved goodbye to Ollie. Even through Toby's terrible times, Katie had always said hello to us – despite the fact that Toby always blanked her.

Now, as she always did, she turned to face him with a wide, inclusive smile. 'And how are you doing, Toby Turner?' she asked.

He looked up at her. 'I'm doing very well now, thank you,' he said, without missing a beat. 'I'm doing very well now that I have my dog – do you know my dog?'

'I've never had the pleasure before—' Katie started to say.

'Well, this is Sox,' Toby interrupted her, so keen was he to talk. 'Sox is a Labrador Retriever Cross but we think there *might* be a touch of Irish Wolfhound in there too because, as you can see, he's a very large dog. He is seventy centimetres tall and over one metre long. He weighs thirty-seven point nine kilos, which makes him a *very* big boy. His birthday is in August, which means he is almost two years old, but not quite. He has a sister called Shannon and he comes all the way from Ireland …'

And he was off. We'd bought Toby some books on dogs, such was his passion for them, and that gave him a *lot* of knowledge about Sox's breed and how you should care for him and all manner of other facts, which he now imparted to Katie with all the gravitas of a TV newsreader. He was just chat, chat, chat, constantly. This was a boy who'd not had conversations with people *ever*. He had never before acknowledged Katie's existence. Now, she was pupil, audience, rapt listener … *there*. She was there, and Toby saw her and made contact. It was something I'd never, ever seen him do.

I took a deep breath, all of a sudden feeling just a little bit wobbly. *This is what it's supposed to be like*, I thought. *This is lovely.*

This is nice. I was so proud of Toby's confidence, his articulate manner, his pleasant way of speaking; his encyclopaedic knowledge of his favourite thing in the world. As I listened to him talking away, I just stood there smiling.

Katie and I exchanged a glance over his head. She looked stunned. Later, she would say to me, 'Vikky, I know Toby, I've spent time with Toby, but I've *never* spoken like this to Toby at all.'

Other people stopped Toby too, on our way home, to ask him about his impressive-looking dog. Sox proved a real talking point. It literally took us hours to walk the fifteen-minute route home, because Toby was pausing and chattering away to everyone we met. It was quite amazing. There were even times when he'd finish a conversation and then think of something else he *had* to say – so we'd have to go back so he could talk to the adult again. It was still only the adults he was speaking to, but my, oh my, *how* he was speaking!

There was one clear message through it all, though. In amongst his prattle about Sox's breed and weight and height and age and heritage, Toby kept saying one thing again and again. Its simplicity said it all. In three brief words, Toby summed the whole thing up. He said: 'Sox helps me.'

It was perhaps the third or fourth weekend after we'd taken Sox home that we really got to see how extraordinary that help could be. Kelly had been careful to advise us not to have big celebrations or anything like that for Sox's arrival; we were told not to invite lots of people round because quiet time, for Toby and Sox both, was of critical importance at this early stage. We had of course followed her advice to the letter. On this weekend, however, we had invited Neil's parents round, just to see how we got on with two visitors.

Toby always found family visits difficult. It was change, you see: a change to his routine; new people (even though they were relatives) in the house. As usually happens with any family gathering, at one point we all found ourselves in the kitchen: the four grown-ups and the four children and Sox. The conversation was flowing and there was a nice burble of happy chatter as we caught up on each other's news.

I don't know exactly what happened. I suspect it all just got a bit busy and maybe Toby couldn't get his word in, and so he just lost it. He roared, a loud roar of frustration, and then he stormed out and stomped all the way upstairs, effing and blinding and shouting. We heard footsteps thundering from his bedroom and his angry cries: 'I'm not coming out! I'm staying here!'

'I'll go,' said Neil. But I laid a hand on his arm.

'Neil,' I said, an idea sparking within me. 'Shall we just send the dog up?'

His green eyes lit up. 'Well, yeah,' he said. 'Shall we give it a go?'

I called Sox over to me and together with Neil the three of us went out into the hallway, where I crouched down to Sox's level.

'My boy needs a bit of calming down, Sox,' I said to him.

Sox looked back at me levelly, his dark eyes taking in the mission. He sat as still as a soldier reporting for duty, and I stroked down his smooth black fur as I asked him for his help. He almost nodded at me, an understanding dip of his onyx muzzle, and then he started padding up the stairs at a nice, calm, sensible pace, just as I'd seen the assistance dog do on that local news VT eighteen months before. This time, it was our staircase he was heading up. It was our boy he was going to save.

Toby had left his bedroom door open. Neil and I tiptoed carefully after Sox and together we crouched on the stairs, out of the way, but with a perfect view of our son in his room.

He was sitting on the bottom bunkbed, his shoulders slumped and his arms crossed angrily across his chest. His blond head was down and he was scuffing moodily at the carpet with one besocked foot.

Sox hesitated in the doorway, as though making an appraisal of the situation. Then, on my command, he boldly entered in and jumped up onto the bed beside Toby in one smooth, graceful leap. He settled down beside his friend and laid his black head on Toby's lap.

Toby didn't react, not at first. But as Neil and I watched from the stairs, holding our breath, we saw one of Toby's hands move from where it was forced angrily into his crossed-arm position. Very, very slowly, still not looking at his dog, he extended that hand in Sox's direction, and started to just sort of rub Sox's fur with his fingers. After a while, that hesitant movement became a steady stroke of his friend's soft side.

We noticed his other hand very, very slowly start to move upwards, until Toby had put his thumb in his mouth to comfort himself and began rhythmically sucking on it. He was stroking Sox with one hand and sucking the thumb of the other, and as we kept on watching we saw him lean against Sox as though the dog was almost bearing him up: taking his weight, and the weight of the world that Toby had felt was upon his shoulders.

Sox was strong enough for them both.

It had taken less than ten minutes, and our angry little boy was now a picture of peace: cuddling his dog, breathing calmly, his body relaxed and his face a tranquil cherub's visage.

Neil and I let out our breath. 'That's amazing,' I whispered to my husband.

'I know,' he whispered back. He squeezed my hand. 'I've never seen Toby calm down so fast.'

'I *know*,' I whispered to him in return. 'He calmed down *so* quickly …'

And then, before Neil and I even had time to move from our hideout on the stairs, Toby almost tumbled over us – as he and Sox came to rejoin the party. Before Sox, Toby would have stayed in his room for the rest of his grandparents' visit; he probably wouldn't even have come downstairs to say goodbye. But with Sox by his side, he felt calm and confident enough to return to our family visit *and* participate in it.

It felt truly miraculous.

But the real miracle was the impact that Sox had not just on Toby, but on the entire Turner family. The whole atmosphere in the house just changed completely. Rather than running along a conveyor belt in the wrong direction, sprinting at top speed just to stay still – which was how things had felt before – now we were all just walking along a road, the seven of us hand in hand, with our shadows growing long on the path beside us, heading calmly into the future. It had been very distressing for the other children to witness Toby's breakdowns – and to experience his rage when he lashed out at them, verbally and physically – but the environment at home now felt safe. We weren't constantly waiting for the next upset to happen; we weren't constantly trying to keep our family from breaking apart. It was as though the whole household breathed a sigh of relief.

Lauren even said to me, a few weeks after Sox's arrival, 'The house feels really happy now. What a huge difference, Mum. Isn't it?'

And it really was. I don't think we'd realised quite how subdued and beaten down we'd been beforehand, but now the change was visceral. Before, we'd been surviving on an hour-by-hour basis – now, we began to be able to make plans.

So we started to test the water a little. We risked a lunch at the local pub. They didn't have what Toby wanted on the menu, but Sox laid his heavy head on Toby's lap to reassure him, and suddenly it didn't matter anymore. Toby popped his thumb in his mouth and stroked his dog and I could see that special Sox calmness come over him, like a warm wet wave or a snuggly, crunchy cotton duvet. After that, the meal went off without a hitch.

One sunny weekend, when the children were all rattling round the house, I suggested to Neil, 'Shall we go for a walk?'

'That's a great idea,' he said. He raised his eyebrows at me, as though challenging me to a dare. 'Shall we go to the forest?'

I even giggled a little bit. 'Why not?' I said. 'Let's try it.'

We pulled up at the forest car park and got out, holding only a rucksack with some dog treats and water bottles in it; not a tent to be seen. Toby and Sox and I walked with the harness across the car park to ensure Toby was safe, but once we were in the woods proper I let Sox off the lead and let him have a free run. He scampered off on his Bambi long legs, kicking up the soil beneath him with his claws. The kids all ran and chased after him, and Sox had a great time running off, pausing so that they could catch up with him – even Ollie on his sturdy little five-year-old legs – and then haring off again at top speed. His pink tongue was lolling out of his mouth and, if dogs could grin, Sox was definitely beaming.

'Mummy, Mummy, can we play hide and seek with Sox?' the kids chorused to me.

'Of course you can!' I said. Neil and I walked behind them, arm in arm, watching our family scamper around the woods.

Lauren got the dog treats out of the rucksack and distributed one to each child.

'OK, *go*!' she cried to her brothers.

And then the children split up and ran to all four corners of the earth. Sox, with his sooty ears pricked up to attention, watched them go. He'd have been after them like a shot – once he'd decided which child to chase – but I told him to wait, ready to release him once the kids were in position.

They each chose their own hiding place behind a bush or a tree or a handily located shrub.

'OK, Sox, go find them,' I said, and I let him free.

His nose went straight to the ground to pick up the scent, and then he lolloped off with tremendous exuberance, his tail wagging nineteen to the dozen as he tore off in the direction of Toby. It wasn't like any silent version of hide and seek you've ever known, because the kids immediately started calling out to him.

'Sox! *Sox*! Over here, Sox! *This* way!'

And Sox ran after each of them, one by one, as they called his name, sniffing out his treats and having a very, very jolly time indeed. Neil and I watched the whole thing with undiluted pleasure, as the kids yelled Sox's name and ran and chased and hid from the dog the whole afternoon. We were all just having a laugh, messing around, and the sunlight was filtering through the trees and casting the kids' faces with this golden glow. Every one of them was smiling. Every one of them was laughing.

Sox had brought the laughter back to my family.

I had never felt so grateful to that big black lovely dog.

21

An Epic Day Out

A letter arrived in the post in June 2013.

> *We are pleased to inform you that Toby Turner has been accepted for a place at St Andrew's School. He will start full-time in September 2013 …*

I breathed a heady sigh of relief. St Andrew's had an autism base attached to the mainstream school – a communication, interaction and language base, they call it – and it was the kind of place we had hoped that Toby would be able to attend. When the students with autism were able to, they integrated into the mainstream state school and joined in, but most of the time they were educated in a safe space with specially trained tutors who were equipped with the knowledge to manage their condition. Yet the decision for Toby to gain a place had to go before a panel and he'd needed to be accepted by all the authorities before it was a done deal, so this letter was the end point of an awful lot of hard work and hope behind the scenes.

I had gone to have a look around the base. The first thing I saw when I got there was that it had a big fence all the way around it, with coded keypads on the gates. *This is the one!* I thought excitedly. *This is where he needs to go because if he has a meltdown he won't be able to get outside the school grounds. He will be safe here, no matter what happens in his day.*

Inside, my impressions of what the base had to offer were even better. Rather than classrooms full of big communal tables, which forced the children to interact, they had little booths for the students to work in, where the tutors could give intimate, one-on-one support. There were no displays on the walls, in fact all the décor was extremely plain, and I immediately understood why. Colourful displays to autistic children are like looking straight at the sun – too stimulating, to the point where it's painful.

Though Toby wouldn't start until the September, the school were excellent about preparing him for the change. One of the teachers from the base came out to our Banbury classroom to introduce herself to him. She brought some photos with her of the other children who attended the base so that Toby could be prepared to meet them.

Toby and I were also invited to attend the base together for a visit. I explained beforehand that the other children there had Asperger's like him and that the school was all sorted out to know how he needed to be taught and looked after. After his experiences at his first school, we had told him that what we needed to do was find him a school that understood his needs and the way his super-autistic brain worked so that he could become anything he wanted to be. In St Andrew's, we were very hopeful we had found it.

And so Tobes and I went for a couple of afternoons that summer term. We didn't take Sox, because he wouldn't be going to school with Toby, but despite his absence Toby was OK and we had some nice visits. While there we met Margaret, who was an older teacher in her fifties with short, curly greying hair. She was a very calm person who spoke only what she needed to; there was no flowery language or hyperbole. I remember at one point during the afternoon she spoke to Toby through a talking tube, like a long pretend telephone, so she was talking in one end and then he would talk in the other, and I thought that was very good; that she was playing with him. Toby really warmed to her. He was so chuffed when I told him that he would be seeing her again and that she would be one of his teachers.

At one point, of course, we did have an issue. I think he said he wanted to make a sword while he was there, because he'd found a helmet in their dressing-up box or something, and I'd said, 'No, we don't make swords,' because I'm very anti-swords and guns and violence, and all the kids know that.

Toby, true to form, harrumphed in a very cross way and stormed out of the classroom. I put down the arts and crafts materials and followed him outside. We had a nice, calm, sensible chat about what had happened and then we went back into the base.

And oh – the teachers' reaction! The first thing they said to me was, 'How did you do that? How did you calm him down?' They wanted to know how I managed him, so they could use the same techniques when I wasn't there in September. That was when I really felt that Toby would be understood there. I felt very lucky that he had managed to get a place; there are only two primary-school bases in our area and each accepts only 10 pupils, so the competition for places was fierce.

Kelly was still checking in with us regularly to ensure that Sox was settling in well. And when she came for a visit towards the end of June I think she could definitely see that he was now one of the family. All of us were thoroughly involved in his care, which is something the charity encourages. Kelly had given us a timetable of all the jobs that needed doing for Sox and we had each taken on a different job to do every day. Because Toby and I have special roles in Sox's eyes, we always do the feeding, but Neil, Joe, Lauren and Ollie divided up the playtime and the bathing and the brushing and all those sorts of things so that the whole family was involved. I was lucky enough to be on 'free run' duty, which meant that every day I got 60 minutes outside in the fresh air, throwing a ball for Sox as he ran and gambolled about. I'm sure it helps all us mums who have assistance dogs, that free-run hour: just a moment of tranquil peace out in nature.

Toby shared his new friend impeccably. The only time he didn't want to share Sox was when he felt he needed him, when he was already in a little place of anger and anxiety. At that point, he would say, 'Sox is mine.' But otherwise, he was quite happy to share Sox, and let Ollie throw his ball for him, or let Joe take him for a run around the field.

As Kelly sat having a cuppa with us in the kitchen, Lauren came down from her room to join us. She was just coming to the end of all her GCSE exams, and my little girl had been as stressed as anything. I was keeping a careful eye on her, given her previous problems with bullying and low self-esteem, but she seemed to be handling the pressure fairly well. Each day when she came home from an exam, she went straight to say hello to Sox, and the two of them would have a play in the garden or a cuddle on the rug in the kitchen. By the time that was done, she was super-calm and ready to get stuck into her evening of revision for the next paper.

As my daughter walked into the kitchen, Sox got to his feet and his tail started to wag. Normally he stood up when any member of the family came in so he could give them a bit of fuss, but I had noticed of late that he had a special spot for Lauren. As I watched the two of them now, I saw Lauren had noticed his movement and was walking towards him to give him a hug. Sox's tail was like a sensor – the closer she got, the faster and faster it wagged, until it was just a fuzzy black blur as she reached him and gave his ears a lovely waggle with both her hands.

'So you were saying that you'd been to the forest and to the pub for lunch?' Kelly prompted, bringing me back to my enthused conversation about how amazing Sox had been. 'And …?' she continued, leaving her question hanging. 'What are you doing next?'

I felt a bit flummoxed. 'Oh, I don't know,' I said. I literally couldn't think of anything. We had been out for lunch and gone for a family walk in the woods – wasn't that enough? Wasn't that paradise? Was there really more to strive for when we'd already achieved such highly valued prizes that, before, would have been completely impossible? I almost scratched my head, completely at a loss. 'What *shall* we do?' I asked her, needing her help.

She gave me one of her sincere, understanding looks. 'You're so used to not doing anything,' she said sympathetically. 'But now you can. You can do *anything*! So just do it. Go for it! Whatever you want, just go and do it. Go and do something as a family. Whatever you like.'

Her words almost made the scales fall from my eyes. *She's right*, I thought, *we really should make some plans.* For so long when the weekends arrived we'd planned nothing, but now the world had started to open up again and we began to think of our weekends: *Where shall we go? What shall we do with these glorious empty days before us that can now be filled with fun?*

Not long after Kelly's visit, I broached the subject over dinner one night. All six of us were sitting round the table, with Sox in his basket nearby. I'd been thinking long and hard about what we might do next, and I thought I had hit on a winner of an idea.

'At the weekend,' I began, 'shall we try going to the Natural History Museum in London again?'

Neil looked at me as if I'd gone mad. His eyes were saying: 'You *what*? You want to do *what*?' But the kids, to my delight, chorused, 'Ooh, yeah! That would be really nice!'

Even Toby joined in. The kids weren't apprehensive at all. I said, maybe to reassure Neil as much as the children, 'We can do anything now we've got Sox.'

I was ecstatic the plan had a green light. Now Kelly had opened up my eyes, going back to the museum was the first thing I'd thought of. I could still remember how enthused the kids had been for the tiny bit of the day that had gone well, and I knew they could have such a good time now that Toby had Sox by his side. There was the potential for us all to completely love it. Each of the kids was a scientist at heart, so it was very much our kind of place.

Neil dusted off the leaflet he'd picked up on the disastrous trip and we all pored over it to pick out which sections of the museum we wanted to visit. The kids needed no encouragement.

'*Dinosaurs!*' roared Toby, like a T-rex himself.

'*Dinosaurs!*' yelled Ollie, his eyes wide as saucers.

'*Dinosaurs!*' shouted Joe, already looking excited.

'*Dinosaurs!*' cried Lauren, completing the set.

'Ooh,' added Toby, piping up with an extra request, 'and can we please go to the coffee bar? Cos the coffee bar's good.'

'Toby Turner,' I said, smiling at him, 'we can go anywhere you want.'

And so that weekend the Turner family retraced its steps. Into the car we went; Sox making the leap from floor to boot with athletic flair. Along the motorway and into the capital we drove, as Sox watched the cars whizzing by and turned his inquisitive eyes this way and that to take everything in. We parked and clambered out, and Sox and Toby and I put on the harness.

As we rounded the corner to the museum, the queue was even longer than the last time we'd been. Lots of people were pushing past and I think Lauren was actually more disturbed than Toby; she doesn't like big busy cities, and because she was the eldest neither Neil nor I was really watching over her.

Together, we surveyed the mass of people. It was huge. And I took an executive decision. As a family, we climbed the steps straight up to the museum door. Sox lolloped up them too, the high-vis flash on his harness shining brightly against his dark fur.

'Excuse me,' I said to the guard. 'I'm afraid we can't queue. Would it be OK to go straight in, please?'

'Yeah, of course you can,' the man replied, and the seven of us were ushered through the doors and into the teeming lobby.

It was as easy as that. We'd never asked for special treatment before – because we didn't feel deserving, I suppose. But with Sox in his special jacket by our sides, for good or bad he gave Toby a label, and people responded accordingly. It wasn't just the guards it affected – we found people gave us more space as we moved through the lobby, which in itself helped Toby not to feel too crushed and claustrophobic. They moved aside and let us through. I liked it, too, because it helped me to know that people weren't judging Toby or our parenting skills on his behaviour. Sox's presence immediately showed people that Toby had additional needs and they in turn were immediately more understanding.

As we gathered in the lobby, as usual there was the collective cry to use the facilities before we started to explore. But Toby was quite happy. It was amazing the difference that both Sox and the lack of a wait had had. People were commenting on Sox all the time ('Ooh, what a lovely dog!') and Toby was proudly chattering away to them, 'Oh yes, he's my dog and he's a Dog for the Disabled because I have autism. Do you know he is seventy centimetres tall and over one metre long …?' However, I noticed Lauren still seemed a bit freaked out by the bustle. It *was* extremely busy.

'Lauren,' I said to her gently. 'I'm just going to take Ollie to the toilet, but I've noticed Sox is looking a bit stressed at the moment. Would you please just go and give him a fuss and reassure him for me?'

Obedient as ever, she went and sat with Sox and started cuddling him. And as Ollie and I fought our way through the crowds, I glanced back to see Sox placing his large black head happily on her lap as she tousled his ears. All the hustle-bustle seemed to fade away and Lauren was calm once more. Sox's magic wasn't just for Toby; he waved his wand for us all.

'Right then,' I said, when we had returned. 'Let's get going.'

And off we went, with Sox and Toby harnessed together and the whole family ready for an adventure. We went straight to the dinosaur section, just as we had planned, and it turned out they had a special exhibition on, which was really quite something. And then, because the day was going well, we did the fossil section too. We even did some of the hands-on interactive bits, which are normally really difficult because people always push through to have a turn. And Toby did complain loudly, 'Why *do* people just keep pushing in?' but he didn't get angry, and he didn't get cross. Instead, we occasionally saw him sigh, and run a steady hand along Sox's broad black back. That was it. Normally, he wouldn't have been able to verbalise his frustration – he would have just got more and more upset and cross and angry – but this time he said what was annoying him, and then he moved on.

In the olden days, before Sox, before we stopped going out, any plan would be a short, sharp visit to get some fun in before Toby had a meltdown. It was always a regimental 'this is what we're doing' – and whatever it was, it was the *only* thing we did; if we were lucky enough to get there at all. But now we planned as we went along.

'OK, we've seen the fossils, what shall we look at next?'

And we'd head along to the space section and spend another half an hour there, and another after that, getting our minds blown by awe-inspiring astronomy.

It was all just *lovely*. We saw everything we wanted to see. We had lunch together and it was completely without incident. Sox was really chilled out; he curled up and had a nap while we ate. To him it really didn't matter where he was, so long as he could catch a few zzzzs every now and then.

After the museum, we went to Hyde Park to give the dog a run round. Sox in London! He chased all the kids all over the green lawns and in and out of the trees. And after that, on the way home, we really tested our limits and went to Frankie and Benny's for tea. They're always noisy and busy, aren't they? But Toby was as good as gold. Sox sat smartly next to him and my son was so relaxed as a result that I didn't even panic when Toby put his order in and the waiter couldn't oblige. We got it sorted and we all had a meal out together … having just had an adventure in London … which lasted all day long. We had never *ever* managed such a long day out before. It was exhausting! But here we were, clinking glasses of soda and saying, 'Cheers!'

'Cheers, Sox!' said Toby happily.

We were just like a normal family.

I tucked Toby up in bed that night, and we chatted about everything we'd done. I'd just tiptoed to the edge of his room when a little voice said, 'Mummy?'

'Yes, Tobes?'

'I had the most epic day *ever*!' he told me.

22

The Last Word

In the final week of the summer term of July 2013, Toby was invited to attend a full week of school at the base, so that it wouldn't be a huge culture shock for him in September. They wanted him to feel prepared to go full-time when he began Year Four after the summer. That week, Neil dropped Ollie off at school for me so that I could take Toby in and get him settled.

'Toby,' I said to him that Monday morning, 'it's time to go to school.'

He was sitting on the sofa in the den. Sox was lying next to him, his heavy head stretched out across Toby's knee. Toby had his thumb in his mouth and his other hand was just stroking his dog, over and over.

Toby took a deep breath, as though steadying himself. 'OK, Mummy,' he said bravely, and he lifted Sox's head from his knee and jumped down from the couch. He bent to give his dog the most enormous cuddle. 'See you after school, Sox,' he whispered to him.

Sox padded after us into the hallway, seeing us off. His steady brown eyes watched Toby solemnly and with maybe a bit of pride, though perhaps that was just me. Toby picked up his schoolbag and his lunch bag, and together we walked out of the house.

As we drove, we had CBeebies music playing on CD. Toby liked music, and I hoped it would be calming for him. I could feel he was a little tense. When we arrived at the base, we walked into his classroom and he was rather reserved, standing back a little bit. But the staff were very welcoming, and Toby seemed to put his worries to one side enough to be able to walk fully into the room and sit down.

'See you later, Tobes,' I said from the doorway. 'Have a good day.'

I went back to the car and drove off. It felt horrible, *really* horrible. After a while I realised I was still listening to the CBeebies CD, and I turned it off. But, actually, the silence was worse.

Toby had always been there at the side of me before. I couldn't help thinking of our long chats where we would put the world to rights as I drove him here and there, my ever-present shadow. Now, there was no one to talk to. It was actually really … lonely. I just remember being lost, in a way.

Not knowing what else to do, I drove into town and went for a look around the shops. I didn't have long before picking up Ollie, and I didn't know how long Tobes would last anyway, so I was just trying to keep myself busy, really. I hadn't been shopping by myself in a very long time yet I was simply killing time; I wasn't doing it because I wanted to and it wasn't even fun. I didn't see the things in the shops – instead, my mind was full of Toby and how he was getting on. All the while I kept checking my phone religiously, worried I had unwittingly gone out of phone signal and the school might be trying to call.

But my phone stayed silent. They didn't ring once.

That afternoon, after four hours away from Toby, I drove back to the base and picked him up.

'Did you have a nice day?' I asked him cautiously. Sometimes even asking about a day, if it had gone badly, could prompt a negative reaction and then hours of repair.

But Toby simply said, 'Yeah, I had a nice day!'

I smiled. 'What did you do?' I asked.

'I can't remember!' he said cheerily.

But whatever it was, he had clearly enjoyed it. It was so lovely. I felt incredibly emotional: we'd found somewhere for him where he could be safe and he could learn, and where he would be looked after too. And he never looked back. From day one he really enjoyed it, and across that week we could see him becoming more and more comfortable. Every morning before school he would sit in the den with Sox and have a cuddle, and every afternoon when he got home, it was the same. Sox was on debrief duty now, and my co-captain on Team Toby was doing a quite exceptional job.

Even when Toby went full-time in September, it was plain sailing. It had been arranged that a taxi would take him to and from school, and Neil and I were quite anxious about that: a new car, a new driver, a new routine … How would Toby cope? We thought perhaps the driver would introduce himself beforehand but he didn't, he just turned up on the first day of term to take our son to school, and Neil and I were so concerned about how Toby would manage.

But Toby just skipped out of the door. 'Bye!' he said breezily. It was absolutely amazing! And as I watched him walk to the car, waving him off from the front window, I could actually see him growing in confidence with every single step. (Neil, in fact, followed the taxi all the way to school, just in case, but it turned out that Toby didn't need him to. As if he'd been doing it all his life, he simply slipped out of the car, cheerily slammed the door and then sauntered into school without a backward glance.)

It was the same when he came home that first afternoon. He rang the doorbell and then announced, '*Hello*! I'm home!' The confidence in him was massive; the difference simply breathtaking. I almost had to remember to breathe – I was so caught up in his transformation. I'd always been aware that if we could get him into the right place at a young age that it could influence his whole life, and now, for the first time, I could see that future life for him, and how much better it was going to be. I think I had tears in my eyes that entire day. Like most mothers, I always mourn my children when they go, and all that day I was partly thinking, *Oh, it's the end of an era* ... But I knew, with great excitement and hope, that it was also a new beginning.

Even buying his school shoes didn't cause a fuss, unlike before. Neil and I took Toby and Ollie on their own to get them, and we were both apprehensive as the four of us and Sox entered the busy shop. Sox plonked his bottom in a corner on the floor, and then lay down fully, with a drowsy, doggy sigh. Toby, following his friend's lead, sat down next to him between Sox's legs, so his back was against the dog's belly. He curled in and put his head on Sox's shoulder, and the pair of them waited patiently like that until the assistant was ready with Toby's shoes.

All the while Neil and I were just looking at each other, our eyes exclaiming, '*What?*! Is this really happening?' Toby was so calm we even went to Burger King afterwards and managed to make a time of it. Neil and I kept exchanging glances the whole afternoon but we didn't say a word about it – because we didn't want to tempt fate.

My husband and I were finding we had more time to be together now, which was just the nicest thing. I had missed him. With Toby at full-time school and it going well, I had much more time to get all my jobs done in the day, meaning the evenings and weekends were less busy and fraught. Neil and I could sit down and have a cup of tea together and talk.

While we were both thrilled about the changes in Toby, I think Neil was also rather pleased about the transformation in *me*. I was far less drained, emotionally, these days. And because I was less stressed, I was far less tired, which meant I could actually hold an intelligent conversation with him. Sometimes, you know, we didn't even talk about the kids. At long last, we were able to get some adult time together. I felt like I was falling in love with him all over again.

Meanwhile, Toby Turner was making a few friends of his own. His best friends at school were now Amanda and Joshua. Their friendships could be up and down, as you can imagine – mortal enemies one day, blood brothers the next. He got on particularly well with Josh, who was a small, dark-haired boy in the same school year as him. Toby tells me he's neither quiet nor loud and that they share the same interests.

Over time, having friends gave Toby more emotional empathy and a clearer perspective on others. We always do 'daily achievements' with the family over supper, and we noticed Toby mentioning Josh more and more often as time went by.

'My achievement for the day,' he would announce when it was his turn to share, 'is that I really helped Josh when he was feeling stressed. I made him feel better.'

Toby was now the one to understand when someone else was having a meltdown, and the one telling them reassuringly, 'It's going to be OK.'

He even made friends with his little brother, who had always tested his patience so greatly by disturbing his neat lines of motorcars and not playing by his rules. But now Toby and Ollie started to play beautifully together – hours-long games of Marvel superheroes and Lego – in what seemed to be quite an equal partnership, although I did sometimes hear Toby taking on the role of big brother. If Ollie pretended to fire a gun at Toby ('Pew pew!' I'd hear from the lounge), Toby would suddenly stop the game and give Ollie a lecture about violence, cribbed from my own frequent admonishments.

'Now, Ollie,' he would say, in a very adult tone, 'violence hurts people. We don't have violence in this household, thank you very much.'

I wholeheartedly approved, of course, but it was also really funny.

And another playmate was Toby's old friend from school, Peter. As Ollie still attended Toby's first school, Peter's mum Julie and I often ran into each other at the school gates. Knowing how fond of Peter Toby was, I invited him over for some playdates, and I was happy that Peter wanted to accept. The two of them would sit in Toby's bedroom on the top bunk, playing with their Nintendo DSs and chatting away.

As I drove Peter home after one of these dates – he and Toby sitting in the back together, two blond pals who had just spent a lovely afternoon together – Peter turned to me and said, 'Mrs Turner? I don't think Toby's got Asperger's anymore.' Toby had been so well behaved and sociable he'd been like a different boy all afternoon.

It was Toby who responded: 'I *do*!'

I simply said, 'Toby's grown up a lot now, Peter.'

For our family, his new mature attitude (and the reason for it: Sox) meant that we could now enjoy experiences we hadn't shared in years. At the start of 2014, when Ollie's Year-One class were full of chatter about the new Disney film, we were able to take him and his siblings to see *Frozen* at the cinema. Toby sat on the end of a row, next to the aisle, with Sox sat right there beside him, and it was such a calm experience. (Notwithstanding, of course, the manic singing-along from a cinema full of sugar-charged six-year-olds!) It was just really cool – we all had such a fantastic time.

And that was only the start of it. We've done some amazing things together: gone into London to see West End shows like *Wicked*, and Sox has even gone for a ride on the London Eye. Now I had hopes for the future – a future that simply hadn't been there before – I was soon back to my old ways of planning every single day of every vacation and filling it up with trips, much to Neil's dismay! The Cotswold Wildlife Park and Gardens, Legoland, the Doctor Who Experience … I always enthused about these ideas to Neil, and he always indulged me. In truth,

I believe we were both just thrilled to be able to give our kids their childhood back. I think it's really important for children to remember doing family things and having fun, and for too long that hadn't happened in our house.

Sometimes, if we were planning to go to a not-necessarily-dog-friendly place, such as a hospital to visit a relative who was sick, we would say to Toby, 'It might be a bit hard with the dog, Tobes. Shall we leave Sox here?'

'No, no,' Toby would say, 'we're taking Sox!'

And that was fine, if that was what Toby needed to feel safe, and so that was what we did. We went to so many places where, afterwards, Neil and I would look at each other and say, 'That would have been impossible before.' But with Sox there, *anything* was possible.

Toby wasn't cured, don't get me wrong. I don't want to give a misleading impression; to his friend Peter or to you. He wasn't cured by a long shot; well, there *is* no cure – and anyway we wouldn't want to change the special person that Toby is. Lauren did her AS-level extended research project on autism and she looked into both the possible cures and causes of the condition. She confessed to finding it a frustrating project, actually: she didn't discover what she wanted to. She'd been looking especially at the causes of autism in the hope that, if you could identify where it began, you'd be in a position to make the puzzle easier to solve; to make finding the solution not quite so daunting. But she said that, as she read academic paper after academic paper on the topic, she realised how very little was known, even after years of professional research.

Lauren was studying biology, chemistry, maths and French for her A levels. She still wants to study medicine long term.

One of her counsellors had previously suggested to her that her passion to become a doctor is rooted in the fact that she'd always wanted to make Toby better – and we both believe it probably is. She spent a lot of her adolescence feeling helpless that she couldn't do anything to help him, and the idea of pursuing a career where she might just be able to after all – where she might just be able to do something to ensure no other child ever has to go through what he went through – is irresistible to her. She makes me very proud, as do all my children. Lauren and Joe and Ollie and Toby – I am so very proud of them all.

So my son wasn't cured, oh no. Toby still had difficult days – days where he would have a strop, days where he would have a meltdown at school for one reason or another. Whenever something did go a little pear-shaped, the school always looked at the reasons why and how they could make it better next time. There was no blame and no 'you need to do it this way', it was simply a shared 'we can make it better'. My phone would occasionally ring with a call from the school, but it would be Toby himself on the line. Usually, he'd be ringing just because he needed to hear my voice. The teachers say you can see a physical difference in him when we speak; he just relaxes. So they know it's a good tool for him that works if he happens to be feeling a bit anxious, and therefore it's a tool that's always available to him in times of need.

From time to time, nevertheless, there would still be particularly difficult days for Toby – days when he would come home with a bite mark on his arm, although, these days, it would have to be something very serious indeed for him to do that to himself. But he did still occasionally have that bad feeling inside him, the one that made him feel like he needed to be punished, and so sometimes – maybe only once or twice a year, if that – I did still see that raised little stone circle on his skin.

But whenever Toby was having a tricky time, he knew exactly whom he needed to make him feel better. On those days when life hadn't gone as well as he wanted it to, I would see him lying next to Sox with his thumb in his mouth, just stroking his dog's ear, and I could palpably witness the therapy that was going on. And by the end of it, it was no longer the end of the world that the day hadn't gone right: it was fine. Tomorrow was a new day, and we could get up and do it all again.

Toby never, ever talked about throwing himself out of the window anymore. I never worried about the locks or heard him cry, 'I want to kill myself!' Thanks to Sox, he seemed to be happy in his own skin now. I think before he felt that he didn't fit and that he was somehow wrong, but now he has a lot more confidence in himself – because he knows *exactly* where he fits ... and it's alongside his big black dog.

Toby once tried to explain their connection to me.

'Mummy,' he said, 'it feels like our hearts are connected. It's like they're connected by a special string, an invisible string, and Sox makes everything better. I love him *so* much.'

And you know what? The feeling was absolutely mutual. It was clear to me in the way Sox lovingly cared for Toby: the way he'd gently rest his heavy head on Toby's lap at the slightest sign of increased tension in my boy, or the way he'd get to his feet and go and stand at Toby's side if he heard my son raise his voice in anger. It was there in the way they played together, fooling about in the garden on so many afternoons after school. Sometimes I'd be standing at the sink, doing the washing-up, and through the patio doors I could hear Toby's tinkling laughter and the *wham* of a ball hitting the fence, and Sox's joyous barks ringing out for the whole neighbourhood to hear. I would know the two pals were having a riot together. And it was really, *really* lovely.

In time, Sox was even able to tell Toby he loved him himself. Through Kelly, we sourced a talking button, which is a plastic square button about five centimetres square, on which you can record messages. Sox and I went to a training session to learn how to use it. Neil and I can record messages on the button such as 'Hello, Toby' or 'I love you'. And when Toby needs him to, Sox can press it with his paw, so it's like Sox is talking to Toby and saying those words. It's brilliant to watch.

They are a double act: Toby and Sox, and Sox and Toby. They go everywhere together. If Toby is simply sitting playing with his Lego, Sox is there by his side. Of course he can't assemble the colourful pieces, but you get the sense he is enjoying the game just as much as his boy.

In time, they even went on to train together. They do Kennel Club Awards at Dogs for the Disabled and, in May 2015, Toby took his bronze award exam. The charity used their training hall for the occasion. Toby had to answer lots of questions and show the examiner that he could groom his dog and carry out a health check and so on. And then he and Sox had to perform: Toby walked him round, indoors and out, and gave different commands, and there were lots of distractions and other dogs everywhere, even treats on the floor, but he and Sox were both calm and focused and they walked round *beautifully*. I'm proud to say they passed with flying colours.

Every time Toby does something with Sox, once again his confidence grows. He kind of puffs out his chest and stands taller and his voice takes on this authoritative tone, because he feels self-assured and poised: ready to take on the world. And, world, you better get ready for Toby Turner.

I think my favourite memory of the two of them together, though, is from the Spring Bank Holiday of 2014, when Toby was nine. We had all gone away in the caravan for a family holiday in Rookesbury Park in Hampshire. It's a beautiful spot: you can park your caravan in this lovely wooded area and walk straight out from your door and across the way there's a nature reserve, right there on your doorstep. We used to buy baby caterpillars and grow them into butterflies and this year we let them go in the reserve. It's a really nice place.

It was a very hot day, this particular day I'm thinking of. Something had set Toby off – I can't even remember what it was now – and he'd had a full-scale meltdown.

'Tobes, we need to take the dog out,' I'd said quickly. 'Come on, off we go!'

Sox and I leapt up and started strolling through the woods to the fenced-in dog-walking area, where I'd be able to let him off the lead. Toby followed behind me, a look like thunder on his face. He would stomp along and then stop, as if to say, 'I'm not coming with you, Mummy, I'm staying *here*!' He'd stamp his feet so hard it was as though he was driving tent poles into the ground: this boy was *not* for moving. But, eventually, just when Sox and I were nearly out of sight, I'd be aware of him uprooting his feet and drawing a little bit nearer again.

It was a bit of a walk to the dog area, and by the time we reached it, Toby was letting the stop-start gaps between us grow fewer and fewer, and the distance between us was closing in.

I entered the dog area and waited for him to draw near enough to hear me speak.

'Hey, Tobes,' I said lightly. 'Would you do me a favour? Would you just throw this tennis ball for me, please?'

At this Toby gave a ginormous sigh as though he had lungs the size of skyscrapers. Moodily, he slouched over to me and pulled the ball I'd brought with me out of my hand. He nestled it in his palm and then reluctantly sent it in an arc, hurling it into the dog-walking field.

Sox was off like a rocket. His long legs tangled together as he overshot the landing point, skidded to a halt and then doubled back to pick up the ball with his jaws. He came trotting back to Toby right away and dropped the ball at his feet.

The meaning was clear: 'Again! *Again!*'

With another great sigh, but a slightly smaller one this time, Toby bent down and picked up the wet tennis ball, and once more sent it soaring into the clear blue sky. Sox raced away, keeping his eyes on the ball. He did an acrobatic jump to catch it in mid-air, landed on his feet and started running back.

'Good one, Sox!' Toby called out, impressed by his friend's capabilities.

Sox dropped the ball at his feet. 'More, please!' said his wagging tail and his happy-go-lucky doggy face.

Toby picked up the ball and threw it with all his might. 'Go get it, Sox!' he cried.

And within those three throws of the tennis ball, my boy was back with me. He followed Sox out into the field and then the two of them were jumping around and running up and down and laughing together.

It was at moments like these, when I saw how well their friendship worked, that I counted my lucky stars: every single one of them, blazing brightly against a night sky as black as Sox's fur. Watching them gambol about on the lush green field, beneath a shining near-summer sun, I knew it was a lovely relationship that was always going to be there.

'Mummy,' my son had once said, 'it feels like our hearts are connected. I love him *so* much.'

And you know what? He wasn't the only one.

As I called the pair of them back in, and we turned and headed towards the caravan to rejoin our family, I thought again of Toby's heartfelt words about his very special dog.

And I think I will give the last word to him. It seems only right, don't you think?

'Sox makes everything better.'

Acknowledgements

There are many people I would like to thank. Pam – for going above and beyond on numerous occasions, for the tissues and the hugs, for never giving up and for trying literally *everything* any of us could think of to help Toby. Thank you to Lorna and Helen, too, for their compassion and unshakeable belief in my son.

Elaine, Sox's puppy socialiser, helped Sox to become the loving, reliable rock he is and we will be forever grateful. Thank you also to Kelly at Dogs For Good for her dedication (including learning about the Greek gods!), for fitting in with our family and for matching us to such a perfect dog. Everyone who supports the charity Dogs for Good also deserves our gratitude, for fund-raising the thousands of pounds that it costs to train the wonderful dogs like Sox, so that they can change lives.

I'd like to thank Kate for helping us to find the words to share our story, and Sara at Ebury for publishing it.

Thank you to my children for being the beautiful young people you are; Daddy and I are so very proud of you all. Thank you also for having a laugh and for being forgiving when we don't get things right; this parenting malarkey is not an exact science. Daddy and I love you so very much.

Last, but never least, thank you to my wonderful husband Neil. Without your unwavering support, nothing would be possible. I will love you always.

Vikky Turner, 2016

"A puppy like me could do so much good."

Hello, my name is Jenna. I'm just a puppy now but I'm learning to be a Dog for Good.

One day with your help I will be a proud working dog and wear a smart green jacket, just like my friend Iggy in the small photo.

One day I might become a highly trained assistance dog helping a disabled person to live independently. Or maybe help a child with autism feel less scared and frustrated. I might even work alongside a specialist handler to help children to fulfil their potential at school.

There are so many ways a puppy like me could learn to change someone's life. But I need your help.

It takes special training to turn clever puppies like Jenna into Dogs for Good.

Please sponsor a puppy today for just £5 a month. Visit dogsforgood.org/puppy or call 01295 759812.

DOGS FOR GOOD
SPONSOR A PUPPY